101 SIMPLE SUPPERS
TRIED-AND-TESTED RECIPES

Hylas Publishing
Publisher: Sean Moore
Creative Director: Karen Prince
Designer: Gus Yoo
Editor: Beth Adelman

First Published in 2003 by *BBC Worldwide Ltd*,
Woodlands,

80 Wood Lane, London W12 0TT All photographs © BBC
Good Food Magazine 2003 and *BBC Vegetarian Good
Food Magazine* 2003

All the recipes contained in this book first appeared in
BBC Good Food Magazine and *BBC Vegetarian Good Food
Magazine*.

Published in the United States by
Hylas Publishing
129 Main Street, Irvington,
New York 10533

Copyright © BBC Worldwide 2002

The moral right of the author has been asserted.

Edited by Gilly Cubitt
Commissioning Editor: Vivien Bowler
Project Editors: Rebecca Hardie and Sarah Miles
Designers: Kathryn Gammon and Annette Peppis
Design Manager: Sarah Ponder
Production Controller: Christopher Tinker

First American Edition published in 2003
02 03 04 05 10 9 8 7 6 5 4 3 2 1

ISBN 1-59258-023-8

Set in Helvetica and ITC Officina Sans

Printed and bound in Italy by LEGO SpA

Color origination by Radstock Reproductions Ltd,
Midsomer Norton

Distributed by St. Martin's Press

101 SIMPLE SUPPERS
TRIED-AND-TESTED RECIPES

Editor-in-chief
Orlando Murrin

Contents

Introduction

Our busy lifestyles mean we have less and less time for cooking. Yet our tastes are becoming more sophisticated. That's why at *BBC Good Food Magazine* we have compiled this delectable collection of simple suppers, bringing you a selection of exciting dishes to liven up your repertoire.

Whether you want Middle Eastern spices or the fresh flavors of the Mediterranean, all our recipes use ingredients that you'll have in your pantry or can find at your local supermarket. They're easy to cook, even for beginners, and won't cost an arm and a leg.

Our culinary teams have made sure preparation is kept to a minimum; in fact, many of these recipes are quick stir fries or one-pot dishes you simply stick in the oven. And each recipe comes with a nutritional breakdown so you can look out for the calorie, fat and salt content.

Before you think you don't have time for cooking, we've ensured most of the dishes, including the *Pizza Baked Potatoes* pictured opposite (see page 52 for the recipe), can be cooked in under 30 minutes. These recipes are serious competition for frozen entrees and takeout—and you'll certainly taste the difference

Orlando Murrin

Editor, *BBC Good Food Magazine*

Conversion tables

NOTES ON THE RECIPES
- Eggs are large, unless stated otherwise.
- Wash all fresh produce before preparation.

OVEN TEMPERATURES

°F	°C	Gas	Fan °C	Oven temp.
225	110	¼	90	Very cool
250	120	½	100	Very cool
275	140	1	120	Cool or slow
300	150	2	130	Cool or slow
325	160	3	140	Warm
350	180	4	160	Moderate
375	190	5	170	Moderately hot
400	200	6	180	Fairly hot
425	220	7	200	Hot
450	230	8	210	Very hot
475	240	9	220	Very hot

APPROXIMATE WEIGHT CONVERSIONS
- All the recipes in this book use American measurements. The charts on this page and the next will help you convert to metric measurements. Conversions are approximate and have been rounded up or down. Follow one set of measurements only; do not mix the two.
- Cup measurements have not been listed here, because they vary from ingredient to ingredient. Please use a kitchen scale to weigh dry/solid ingredients.
- Where a recipe calls for a can of something (for example, tuna or tomatoes), we have listed what is generally a standard size can. If the standard cans in your area are a slightly different size, a small difference should not affect the outcome of the recipe.

SPOON MEASURES

• Spoon measurements are level unless otherwise specified.

• 1 teaspoon = 5ml

• 1 tablespoon = 15ml

• 1 Australian tablespoon = 20ml (cooks in Australia should measure 3 teaspoons where 1 tablespoon is specified in a recipe)

APPROXIMATE LIQUID CONVERSIONS

US	Metric	Imperial	Australia
¼ cup	50ml	2fl oz	¼ cup
½ cup	125ml	4fl oz	½ cup
¾ cup	175ml	6fl oz	¾ cup
1 cup	225ml	8fl oz	1 cup
1¼ cups	300ml	10fl oz/½ pint	½ pint
2 cups/1 pint	450ml	16fl oz	2 cups
2½ cups	600ml	20fl oz/1 pint	1 pint
1 quart	1 litre	35fl oz/1¾ pints	1¾ pints

To make the croutons, toss bread cubes in oil and bake in a hot oven for 10–12 minutes until crisp, topping with cheese halfway through.

Vegetable and Cheese Soup

1oz butter
1 tbsp olive oil
1 onion, chopped
1 potato, about 8oz, chopped
2 stalks celery, chopped
1lb 4oz mixed root vegetables,
such as potatoes, turnips,
parsnips and carrots, chopped
salt & pepper to taste
3½ cups vegetable stock
5oz sharp cheddar cheese
1 tbsp wholegrain mustard
cheese croutons, to serve

Takes 50 minutes • Serves 4

1 Heat the butter and oil in a large pot. Add the onion and cook until golden. Add the other vegetables and stir. Season with salt and pepper, cover, reduce the heat and cook for 10 minutes, stirring occasionally, until just tender.
2 Pour the stock into the pan, bring to a boil, then cover and simmer for 20 minutes until the vegetables are softened. Process the soup in a food processor until smooth. Meanwhile, grate half the cheese and cut the rest into small cubes.
3 Reheat the soup in the pot and stir in most of the grated cheese and all the cubes, until the cheese begins to melt. Stir in the mustard and season. Sprinkle with cheese croutons and the remaining cheese.

• Per serving: 320 calories, protein 13g, carbohydrate 21g, fat 21g, saturated fat 11g, fiber 4g, added sugar none, salt 1.78g

Use a jar of satay (peanut) sauce
as a base to make this simple soup.

Vegetable Satay Soup

1lb new potatoes
1 carrot
6oz green beans
1 vegetable stock cube
4oz fava beans in the pod
(or frozen or canned)
12oz jar satay sauce
6oz cherry tomatoes, halved
pita bread, to serve

Takes 20 minutes • Serves 4

1 Cut the potatoes into 1-inch chunks (no need to peel). Quarter the carrot lengthwise, then cut across into small pieces. Trim the green beans, then cut into short sticks.
2 Put the potatoes and carrot in a medium pot with 3 cups of water and the stock cube. Bring to a boil, stir to dissolve the cube, then simmer, covered, for 10–12 minutes until the vegetables are almost tender. Add the green and fava beans and simmer for 2 minutes.
3 Pour in the satay sauce and simmer for 3–4 minutes. Stir in the tomatoes. Serve with warm pita bread.

• Per serving: 596 calories, protein 19g, carbohydrate 40g, fat 42g, saturated fat 9g, fiber 10g, added sugar 6g, salt 3.27g

This is a really light, subtle soup with fresh, vibrant flavors. Serve it without the rice as a starter.

Hot and Sour Coconut Soup

4oz jasmine rice
1 quart chicken or vegetable stock
1 stalk lemongrass, thinly sliced
1 tbsp finely chopped fresh ginger
4 fresh or freeze-dried kaffir lime leaves, chopped or crumbled
2 red chilies, seeded and finely chopped
9oz boneless, skinless chicken breast, thinly sliced
6oz mushrooms, sliced
8oz cherry tomatoes, halved
1 tbsp lime juice
2 tbsp Asian fish sauce (*nam pla*)
7oz sweetened condensed coconut milk
handful of fresh coriander, chopped

Takes 30 minutes • Serves 4

1 Cook the rice in salted boiling water for about 10 minutes, until tender, then drain and set aside.
2 Meanwhile, heat the stock in a large pot, add the lemongrass, ginger, lime leaves and chilies and simmer for 5 minutes. Add the chicken and mushrooms and simmer 5 minutes more.
3 Stir in the tomatoes, lime juice, fish sauce and coconut milk and simmer for 5 minutes more. Scatter the coriander on top and serve each portion with a little cooked rice spooned in.

• Per serving: 356 calories, protein 22g, carbohydrate 26g, fat 19g, saturated fat 15g, fiber 1g, added sugar none, salt 2.47g

It's worth buying mozzarella made from
buffalo milk, not cow's milk, for this salad.

Tricolor Salad with Lemon Dressing

8oz buffalo mozzarella
2 large, firm, ripe tomatoes
2oz arugula

FOR THE DRESSING
½ lemon
good pinch of sea salt
½ tsp freshly ground black pepper
4 tbsp extra virgin olive oil

Takes 20 minutes • Serves 4

1 Cut the mozzarella and tomatoes into slices of equal thickness. Arrange alternate slices of mozzarella and tomato on four plates. Put a pile of arugula beside each.
2 Peel the lemon using a lemon zester to make small, thin strips of peel. (If you don't have a zester, use a potato peeler or a sharp knife to peel off strips of the skin, taking care not to include any white pith, then cut the strips into matchstick shreds.) Squeeze the juice from the lemon into a bowl and add the sea salt and black pepper. Whisk, gradually mixing in the olive oil, until the dressing is thickened.
3 Drizzle the lemon dressing over the arugula, mozzarella and tomato on the plates, garnish with the lemon peel shreds and serve.

• Per serving: 260 calories, protein 14g, carbohydrate 3g, fat 22g, saturated fat 8g, fiber 1g, added sugar none, salt 1.04g

There's no need to cook the couscous—
just soak it and mix in the tasty bits.

Mediterranean Couscous Salad

8oz couscous
14fl oz vegetable stock
10 sundried tomatoes, quartered
2 medium avocados, peeled, pitted
and cut into large chunks
4oz black olives
good handful of nuts, such as pine
nuts, cashews or almonds
8oz feta cheese, roughly crumbled
salt & pepper to taste
5oz mixed lettuce leaves

FOR THE DRESSING
5 tbsp olive oil
2 tbsp lemon juice

Takes 20 minutes • Serves 4
(easily halved)

1 Put the couscous into a large bowl, stir in the stock, cover and leave to soak for 10 minutes.
2 Make the dressing by whisking together the olive oil, lemon juice and seasoning. Stir 2 tablespoons of dressing into the couscous, then gently mix in the tomatoes, avocados, olives, nuts and feta. Taste for seasoning.
3 Toss the salad leaves with the remaining dressing, divide among four plates and spoon the couscous on top.

• Per serving: 636 calories, protein 14g, carbohydrate 29g, fat 52g, saturated fat 11g, fiber 4g, added sugar none, salt 3.82g

Crisp and tangy, chicory adds a soft bite to salads.
Just pull off the leaves and discard the center stems.

Cheddar and Chicory Salad

FOR THE DRESSING
5 tbsp olive oil
2 tsp honey
1 tbsp wholegrain mustard
2 tbsp lemon juice
salt & pepper to taste

FOR THE SALAD
8oz chicory
1 red apple (any variety)
3oz walnut pieces
4oz sharp cheddar cheese

Takes 20 minutes • Serves 4

1 To make the dressing, put all the ingredients into a small bowl and blend thoroughly with a small whisk or fork. Season to taste and set aside.
2 Separate the chicory leaves and divide among four plates. Cut the apple into quarters, core and thinly slice. Scatter the apple slices over the chicory and sprinkle with the walnuts.
3 Using a vegetable peeler, make cheddar shavings and scatter over each serving. Drizzle the dressing over the salad and finish with a grating of fresh black pepper.

• Per serving: 441 calories, protein 10g, carbohydrate 9g, fat 38g, saturated fat 9g, fiber 2g, added sugar 2g, salt 0.59g

Ciabatta (Italian for "slipper") is crusty on the outside, light on the inside. You'll find Caesar dressing in most supermarkets.

Warm Caesar-style Salad

6 medium eggs
5oz green beans, trimmed
1 loaf ciabatta bread
2 tbsp extra virgin olive oil
2oz parmesan cheese, finely grated,
plus extra shavings to garnish
1 romaine lettuce, roughly chopped
salt & pepper to taste
bottled Caesar dressing

Takes 30 minutes • Serves 4

1 Preheat the broiler. Bring a pot of water to a boil, carefully drop in the eggs and cook for 4 minutes. Place in cold water to cool. Cook the green beans in lightly salted boiling water for 4 minutes until tender. Drain well and place in a large salad bowl.
2 Cut the ciabatta loaf into large cubes and toss in the oil and grated parmesan. Spread the bread on a baking tray and broil, turning often, until golden.
3 Peel the eggs and cut into quarters. Add the bread croutons and lettuce to the green beans. Season with salt and pepper and mix well. Pile onto serving plates and top with the eggs. Drizzle with dressing and top with the parmesan shavings.

• Per serving: 684 calories, protein 27g, carbohydrate 67g, fat 36g, saturated fat 8g, fiber 4g, added sugar none, salt 2.68g

This colorful salad travels well in a lunchbox.
Try other beans and cheeses in combination, too.

Cannellini Bean Salad

1 small red onion
1 red or yellow pepper
15oz can cannellini or navy beans
4 tbsp bottled vinaigrette
salad dressing
½ iceberg or 1 romaine lettuce
8oz feta cheese
black pepper
warm Italian bread, to serve

Takes 10 minutes • Serves 4

1 Halve and finely slice the onion and pepper. Drain and rinse the beans. Put the ingredients in a salad bowl.
2 Add the vinaigrette and mix well. Tear the lettuce leaves straight into the bowl.
3 Break the feta into chunks, throw into the salad and season with black pepper. Serve with warm Italian bread.

• Per serving: 348 calories, protein 16g, carbohydrate 17g, fat 25g, saturated fat 10g, fiber 4g, added sugar none, salt 2.57g

A jar of feta cheese cubes marinated in olive oil provides
the protein and the salad dressing.

Chickpea and Feta Salad

1 cucumber, thickly sliced
1 small red onion, thinly sliced
10oz feta cheese cubes
marinated in oil
4 large tomatoes, cut into wedges
15oz can chickpeas, drained
and rinsed
few black olives
juice of ½ lemon
salt & pepper to taste
2 small heads Boston lettuce

TO SERVE
4 pita breads
1 scallion, chopped

Takes 15 minutes, plus draining • Serves 4

1 Put the cucumber and onion in a strainer over a
bowl, sprinkle with salt and leave to drain for 20
minutes. Drain the feta cheese cubes, reserving the
oil.
2 Preheat the broiler. Toss the cucumber and onion
with the tomatoes, chickpeas, olives, cheese, 3
tablespoons of the oil and the lemon juice. Season
with salt and pepper. Line salad bowls with the
lettuce leaves and pile the salad on top.
3 Broil the pita on one side, turn over and brush
with a little oil from the cheese. Sprinkle with the
scallion and broil until crisp. Serve with the salad.

• Per serving: 637 calories, protein 28g, carbohydrate 67g, fat
31g, saturated fat 11g, fiber 8g, added sugar none, salt 4.37g

With the main ingredients bought already cooked,
you've only got the potatoes to do.

Warm Mackerel and Beet Salad

1lb new potatoes, cut into
bite-size pieces
3 smoked mackerel fillets, skinned
8oz cooked beets
2oz mixed salad greens
2 celery stalks, finely sliced
2oz chopped walnuts

FOR THE DRESSING
3 tbsp walnut oil
2 tbsp sunflower oil
2 tbsp fresh lemon juice
2 tsp creamed horseradish sauce
salt & pepper to taste

Takes 20 minutes • Serves 4
(easily halved)

1 Cook the potatoes in salted boiling water for 12–15 minutes, until just tender. Meanwhile, flake the mackerel fillets into large pieces. Cut the beets into bite-size chunks.

2 Drain the potatoes and cool slightly. Mix together all the dressing ingredients and season with salt and pepper. Add the potatoes.

3 Add the salad leaves, mackerel, beets, celery and walnuts. Pour on the dressing and toss well. Serve warm.

• Per serving: 634 calories, protein 22g, carbohydrate 26g, fat 50g, saturated fat 2g, fiber 4g, added sugar none, salt 1.91g

This recipe is easily multiplied to feed
a crowd as part of a buffet.

Oriental Shrimp and Pasta Salad

4oz fresh beansprouts
9oz fresh tagliatelle
2 carrots, cut into thin sticks
1 bunch scallions, cut into shreds
¼ cucumber, cut into thin ribbons
with a potato peeler
8oz cooked, peeled shrimp
5 tbsp sunflower oil
2 tbsp light soy sauce
2 tbsp rice wine vinegar or
white wine vinegar
1 tbsp finely chopped fresh ginger
1 large garlic clove, crushed
1 tsp honey
sesame oil, to serve

Takes 30 minutes • Serves 4

1 Put the beansprouts in a bowl, cover with cold water and leave for 10 minutes, then drain (this crisps them up). Meanwhile, cook the pasta in a pot of salted boiling water according to the package instructions.

2 Drain the pasta in a colander and run under cold tap water, then drain thoroughly. Toss with the carrots, spring onions, cucumber, shrimp and beansprouts.

3 For the dressing, whisk together the sunflower oil, soy sauce, vinegar, ginger, garlic and honey. Pour over the pasta and lightly toss. Drizzle with a little sesame oil to serve.

• Per serving: 439 calories, protein 21g, carbohydrate 54g, fat 17g, saturated fat 2g, fiber 4g, added sugar 1g, salt 3.42g

The green bean season is short, so make the most of it. Buy the beans on the day you intend to eat them, if possible.

Green Bean and Bacon Salad

1lb green beans,
cut into fine slivers
4oz good quality bacon,
cut into strips
2 tbsp red or white wine vinegar
4 tbsp extra virgin olive oil
1 tbsp wholegrain mustard
5oz cherry tomatoes, halved,
or small tomatoes, cut into
wedges
salt & pepper to taste

Takes 20 minutes • Serves 4

1 Blanch the green beans in a large pot of salted boiling water for 3 minutes, then drain and cool under cold running water. Drain well and transfer to a serving bowl.
2 Heat a frying pan, add the bacon and let it sizzle until crisp. Remove from the pan and set aside. Drain off some of the fat, then stir the vinegar and oil into the hot pan and warm through. Whisk in the mustard. Pour the warm dressing over the beans.
3 Toss in the tomatoes, then season well with salt and pepper. Garnish with the crispy bacon and serve warm.

• Per serving: 204 calories, protein 6g, carbohydrate 5g, fat 18g, saturated fat 4g, fiber 3g, added sugar none, salt 1.22g

Choose a soft, ripe camembert and
let it rest at room temperature before using.

Bacon and Camembert Salad

8 slices smoked bacon
4–5oz camembert cheese
2 thick slices bread (3oz),
crusts removed
7 tbsp olive oil
5oz mixed salad greens
2 tbsp white wine vinegar
1 tbsp wholegrain mustard
1 garlic clove, finely chopped

Takes 15 minutes • Serves 4

1 Cook the bacon for 5–8 minutes until crisp, turning halfway through. Set aside to cool. Cut the camembert into bite-size wedges.
2 Grate the bread into coarse crumbs. Heat two tablespoons of the oil in a frying pan and cook the crumbs, stirring, until crisp and golden. Season and set aside.
3 Put the salad greens in a bowl. Break the bacon into bite-size pieces and mix into the salad with the cheese. Mix together the vinegar, mustard, garlic and remaining olive oil. Pour over the salad and toss well. Sprinkle with the crisp crumbs and serve.

• Per serving: 465 calories, protein 17g, carbohydrate 12g, fat 39g, saturated fat 12g, fiber 1g, added sugar none, salt 2.56g

Buy a thick slice of ham from the
deli counter for a chunky finish.

Peach, Ham and Cheese Salad

1 romaine lettuce, trimmed and
roughly torn
1 bunch watercress, trimmed
2 peaches, pitted and
cut into thin wedges
4oz edam cheese, rind removed
and cut into sticks
4oz ham, cut into sticks
warm crusty bread, to serve

FOR THE DRESSING
3 tbsp olive oil
1 tbsp white wine vinegar
1 tsp Dijon mustard
2 tbsp mayonnaise
1 tsp honey
salt & pepper to taste

Takes 25 minutes • Serves 4

1 Toss the lettuce, watercress, peaches, cheese and
ham together in a large salad bowl.
2 Whisk together the dressing ingredients and season to taste with salt and pepper.
3 Toss the salad with the dressing just before
serving. Serve with plenty of warm, crusty bread.

• Per serving: 286 calories, protein 12g, carbohydrate 7g, fat
23g, saturated fat 7g, fiber 3g, added sugar none, salt 1.63g

Buy a bottle of honey-mustard dressing,
or mix up your own version.

Chicken Salad with Honey Dressing

1lb new potatoes, scrubbed
and quartered lengthwise
6oz green beans, trimmed
6 slices bacon
4oz mixed salad greens
4 cooked chicken breasts, skinned
and cut into chunks, or about
1lb 9oz cooked chicken
honey-mustard salad dressing

Takes 40 minutes • Serves 4

1 Cook the potatoes in salted boiling water for 8–10 minutes. Add the beans to the water and cook 3 minutes more, until just tender. Drain, cool quickly under cold running then cool completely.

2 Meanwhile, cook the bacon until crispy. Cool, then break into small pieces.

3 Scatter the salad leaves, potatoes and beans over a large serving plate. Toss the chicken with the dressing to taste, then spoon over the salad leaves. Scatter the crispy bacon over the salad and serve.

• Per serving: 505 calories, protein 42g, carbohydrate 26g, fat 27g, saturated fat 5g, fiber 3g, added sugar 6g, salt 2.02g

An easy salad to put together, and it's versatile too.
Try it with shrimp instead of chicken.

Pesto, Chicken and Potato Salad

1lb 2oz new potatoes, unpeeled
12oz skinned, cooked chicken
(about 3 breasts), cut into chunks
4oz baby spinach leaves
2 tbsp pesto
juice of 1 small lemon
3 tbsp olive oil
salt & pepper to taste

Takes 25 minutes • Serves 4

1 Drop the potatoes into a pot of salted boiling water and boil for 15 minutes. Drain, then return them to the pot and roughly crush with a fork.
2 Add the chunks of chicken to the pot and scatter in the spinach leaves. Mix gently, using a large spoon.
3 Mix together the pesto, lemon juice and olive oil, then add to the pot. Season to taste with salt and pepper and toss to coat everything with the dressing.

• Per serving: 365 calories, protein 27g, carbohydrate 21g, fat 20g, saturated fat 5g, fiber 2g, added sugar none, salt 0.39g

Try this with radicchio, frisée, watercress or arugula—
the bitter flavors are great with sweet red peppers.

Leaf Salad with Griddle Chicken

4 boneless, skinless chicken
breasts, each cut into 7–8 slices
2 red peppers, seeded and
cut into strips
3 tbsp olive oil, plus extra
for tossing
salt & pepper to taste
juice of 1 lemon
5oz sour cream
6oz mesclun salad

Takes 25 minutes • Serves 4

1 Heat a large griddle or frying pan. In a bowl, toss together the chicken, peppers, a little oil, some salt and pepper and a little of the lemon juice.
2 Cook the chicken and peppers in batches, in one layer in the hot pan, for 5–8 minutes. Turn them halfway through until the chicken is cooked and the peppers are slightly charred. Allow to cool.
3 Mix together the remaining lemon juice and the sour cream. Whisk in the 3 tablespoons of oil and season. Put the salad leaves in a bowl. Add the chicken and peppers, pour over the dressing, toss lightly and serve.

• Per serving: 331 calories, protein 36g, carbohydrate 7g, fat 18g, saturated fat 6g, fiber 2g, added sugar none, salt 0.26g

Get everything ready, then sizzle the bacon and
livers as guests sit down for a quick lunch or supper.

Warm Chicken Liver Salad

15oz roasted peppers in olive oil,
drained and cut into strips
3oz loose leaf lettuce
(such as lamb's lettuce)
1oz all-purpose flour
14oz chicken livers, thinly sliced
4 thick slices bacon,
coarsely chopped
2 tbsp olive oil
2 tsp red wine vinegar
black pepper

Takes 15 minutes • Serves 4

1 Toss the strips of pepper with the lettuce and
divide into piles among four plates. Season the flour
and use it to coat the chicken livers.
2 Heat a frying pan and add the chopped bacon. fry
until crisp, then remove and set aside on paper
towels. Pour off most of the bacon fat, heat the oil in
the pan and fry the chicken livers for 30 seconds to
1 minute on each side. Remove from the heat and
stir in the red wine vinegar.
3 Arrange the chicken livers on the lettuce and
peppers. Scatter with bacon, drizzle on the dressing
from the pan, season with black pepper and serve
immediately.

• Per serving: 257 calories, protein 23g, carbohydrate 7g, fat
15g, saturated fat 4g, fiber 1g, added sugar none, salt 1g

A French speciality—a toasted ham and cheese
sandwich that's perfect as a snack.

Croque Monsieur

2 thick slices crusty bread
butter, for spreading
2–3 slices thinly sliced ham
25g/1oz gruyère or cheddar
cheese, grated
4 tsp freshly grated
parmesan cheese
salad greens, to serve

Takes 10 minutes • Serves 1

1 Preheat the broiler. Butter the bread and make a
sandwich with the ham and gruyère or cheddar.
Press down firmly.
2 Spread butter over the top of the sandwich and
sprinkle with half the parmesan, then toast under a
moderate broiler until the bread is crisp and the
cheese is browned.
3 Turn over an repeat on the other side. Cut in half
and serve hot with a green salad.

• Per serving: 533 calories, protein 25g, carbohydrate 51g, fat
27g, saturated fat 16g, fiber 2g, added sugar none, salt 2.97g

If you prefer, heat the beans in a pan
and grill the cheese-topped chips.

Tortilla Chips with Cheese and Salsa

2 tomatoes, quartered
½ small red onion, quartered
juice of ½ lime or lemon
4–5 drops Tabasco
2 tbsp tomato paste
salt & pepper to taste
5oz tortilla chips
8oz can refried beans
3oz sharp cheddar cheese, grated
5oz sour cream, to serve

Takes 10 minutes • Serves 2
(easily doubled)

1 Put the tomatoes, onion, lime or lemon juice and
Tabasco in a food processor and process briefly until
finely chopped. Stir in the tomato paste and season
with salt and pepper.
2 Divide the tortilla chips between two microwave-
able plates. Spoon the beans into the center of each
plate, then top with the salsa.
3 Sprinkle the cheese over everything, then
microwave on High, one plate at a time, for 2½ minutes. Serve with sour cream and extra Tabasco, if
you like.

• Per serving: 784 calories, protein 26g, carbohydrate 72g, fat
46g, saturated fat 17g, fiber 6g, added sugar none, salt 3.8g

A cheap and easy family supper.
Make a vegetarian version by omitting the ham.

Cheese and Onion Potato Wedges

4 baking potatoes, cut into
thick wedges
1 red pepper
bunch of scallions
4oz cheddar cheese
4oz thinly sliced ham
salt & pepper to taste
1 tsp paprika
6oz crème fraîche (or cream
mixed with 1/2 tsp buttermilk)

Takes 30 minutes • Serves 4

1 Preheat the broiler to high. Cook the potato
wedges in a large pot of salted boiling water for 15
minutes until tender.
2 Meanwhile, seed and thinly slice the pepper, chop
the scallions and grate the cheese. Drain the
potatoes well, then mix with the red pepper, scallions
and ham. Transfer to a heatproof dish. Season well
with salt and pepper, and sprinkle with paprika. Broil
for 3 minutes until golden brown.
3 Spoon over the crème fraîche, sprinkle with the
cheese and broil for 2–3 minutes more, until the
cheese has melted and the crème fraîche has made
a sauce.

• Per serving: 456 calories, protein 18g, carbohydrate 41g, fat
26g, saturated fat 14g, fiber 4g, added sugar none, salt 1.36g

These potatoes are cooked in the microwave for speed.
Vary the filling according to what's in the refrigerator.

Pizza Baked Potatoes

4 baking potatoes
2 tomatoes
2 × 5oz balls mozzarella
4 small ham slices
4 fresh rosemary sprigs
olive oil, for drizzling
salt & pepper to taste

Takes 25 minutes • Serves 4

1 Wash the potatoes and prick them all over with a fork. Cook in the microwave on High for 10–12 minutes, turning halfway through, until cooked.
2 Preheat the broiler. Slice each tomato and each mozzarella ball into six pieces. Tear each ham slice into three strips. Cut three vertical slits in each potato and stuff each with a slice of cheese, ham and tomato. Tuck a rosemary sprig in the central slit.
3 Drizzle on a little oil and season with salt and pepper. Broil for about 5 minutes, until the cheese has melted.

• Per serving: 421 calories, protein 28g, carbohydrate 32g, fat 21g, saturated fat 11g, fiber 3g, added sugar none, salt 2.36g

A rich alternative to everyday cauliflower,
with a crisp almond topping.

Cauliflower with Stilton Cheese

1 large cauliflower
2oz blanched almonds

FOR THE SAUCE
1oz butter
2 tbsp all-purpose flour
3 cups milk
1 tsp dry mustard
3oz stilton cheese (or bleu cheese or
gorgonzola), plus 1oz
more for sprinkling
salt & pepper to taste

Takes 25 minutes • Serves 4

1 Divide the cauliflower into florets and discard all inedible parts. Steam for 10 minutes until just tender. Meanwhile, preheat the broiler. Halve the almonds lengthwise and toast under the broiler for 4–5 minutes, turning halfway through, until browned.

2 To make the sauce, put all the ingredients (including the cheese) in a wide pan and season with salt and pepper. Heat gently and bring to a boil, whisking all the time, then simmer for 2 minutes, stirring constantly. Season carefully (go easy on the salt).

3 Put the cauliflower in a wide heatproof serving dish and sprinkle with half the toasted almonds. Top with the sauce, remaining almonds and the rest of the cheese. Broil for 5–10 minutes until the cheese is brown and bubbling.

• Per serving: 366 calories, protein 17g, carbohydrate 17g, fat 26g, saturated fat 11g, fiber 4g, added sugar none, salt 1.1g

Choose large flat mushrooms for
stuffing with cheesy mashed potatoes.

Cheese-stuffed Mushrooms

4 large or 8 medium flat mushrooms
3 tbsp olive oil
2 large starchy potatoes
4 or 8 slices bacon
4oz soft cheese with garlic
and herbs

Takes 25 minutes • Serves 4

1 Preheat the oven to 400°F. Wipe the mushrooms
clean. Put them in an ovenproof dish, drizzle with the
oil and bake for 15–20 minutes.
2 Meanwhile, cut the potatoes into small cubes,
then cook in a pot of salted boiling water for 8–10
minutes until just tender.
3 Heat a frying pan and cook the bacon until crisp.
Drain the potatoes, return to the pot and spoon in
the cheese. Mix together lightly, then season. Pile
the mixture on top of the mushrooms and top with
the bacon.

• Per serving: 392 calories, protein 14g, carbohydrate 22g, fat
28g, saturated fat 5g, fiber 3g, added sugar none, salt 1.58g

Cut the bread from a nice loaf,
a few days old, for the best texture.

Cheese and Mustard Bake

6oz sharp cheddar cheese,
finely grated
2 tsp Dijon or English mustard
3 cups 2% milk
salt & pepper to taste
1oz butter, at room temperature
5 thick slices white bread
3 eggs
4 thick slices bacon
Worcestershire sauce, to serve

Takes 50 minutes • Serves 4

1 Preheat the oven to 350°F. Mix together most of
the cheese, the mustard and 3 tablespoons of the
milk. Season with salt and pepper. Butter the bread.
Spread each slice with the cheese mixture. Cut each
slice into four triangles. Butter a 2-quart ovenproof
dish and arrange the bread in the dish with the
points sticking up.
2 Beat together the remaining milk and eggs, and
season with salt and pepper. Pour the liquid over the
bread. Sprinkle with the remaining cheese. Bake for
35 minutes until risen and golden.
3 Meanwhile, cook the bacon for 8–10 minutes until
crispy, turning halfway through. Break into pieces
and scatter over the cheese bake. Sprinkle with a
little Worcestershire sauce and serve immediately.

• Per serving: 569 calories, protein 31g, carbohydrate 36g, fat
35g, saturated fat 19g, fiber 1g, added sugar none, salt 2.94g

The addition of potatoes, leeks and shrimp
makes a meal of scrambled eggs.

Spanish-style Scrambled Eggs

2 medium potatoes
1 leek
3 tbsp olive oil
1 garlic clove, chopped
4 eggs
3 tbsp milk
salt & pepper to taste
4oz peeled shrimp,
defrosted if frozen
Tabasco, to serve (optional)

Takes 25 minutes • Serves 2

1 Cut the potatoes into small cubes (no need to peel). Slice the leek finely. Heat the oil in a frying pan, add the potatoes and saute for about 10 minutes, until they are just tender.

2 Stir in the leek and garlic and cook 5 minutes more, until softened.

3 Beat together the eggs, milk and salt and pepper. Stir the shrimp into the pan. Add the eggs and cook gently, stirring, until scrambled. Serve piping hot, sprinkled with Tabasco.

• Per serving: 468 calories, protein 28g, carbohydrate 25g, fat 29g, saturated fat 6g, fiber 3g, added sugar none, salt 1.16g

A delicious combination of tender asparagus,
creamy sauce and crispy crumbs.

Asparagus Carbonara

knob of butter
1 small onion, chopped
2 garlic cloves, finely chopped
8oz ham, cut into chunks
1lb 5oz asparagus spears
2 eggs
5oz cream
4 tbsp freshly grated
parmesan cheese
salt & pepper to taste
85g/3oz fresh white breadcrumbs
2 tbsp olive oil
2 tbsp finely chopped fresh parsley

Takes 30 minutes • Serves 4

1 Melt the butter in a small frying pan, then cook the onion, garlic and ham for 5–10 minutes until golden. Meanwhile, cook the asparagus in a pot of salted boiling water for 3–4 minutes until just tender. Drain.

2 Whisk together the eggs, cream and 3 tablespoons of the parmesan. Stir in the onion mixture and season with salta nd pepper. In a separate bowl, mix together the breadcrumbs, olive oil, parsley and remaining parmesan.

3 Preheat the broiler. Toss the asparagus with the cream mixture. Pour into a gratin dish and sprinkle the breadcrumb mixture over the top. Broil 2–3 minutes, until the breadcrumbs are golden and the carbonara sauce is hot.

• Per serving: 381 calories, protein 25g, carbohydrate 21g, fat 22g, saturated fat 9g, fiber 4g, added sugar none, salt 2.07g

You could use leftover cooked pasta in this recipe.
Be sure to drain the spinach well.

Pasta and Spinach Tortilla

3oz pasta shells
1lb fresh spinach
8 eggs
4oz sharp cheddar cheese,
coarsely grated
8oz cherry tomatoes, halved
salt & pepper to taste
1 tbsp olive oil

Takes 25 minutes • Serves 4

1 Cook the pasta in salted boiling water. drain.
Wash the spinach well, then put in a pot with just
the water that clings to it and a little salt. Place over
medium heat. When the spinach starts to steam,
cover and cook for 3–4 minutes, until just wilted.
Drain the spinach well, then roughly chop. Mix into
the pasta.
2 Lightly beat the eggs and mix into the pasta with
three-quarters of the cheese and the tomatoes.
Season with salt and pepper. Preheat the broiler.
Heat 1 tablespoon of olive oil in a large frying pan
and cook the pasta and egg mixture for 8–10 minutes, until almost set.
3 Sprinkle the omelette with the remaining cheese,
then broil to brown the top. Serve warm or cold, cut
into wedges.

• Per serving: 361 calories, protein 25g, carbohydrate 19g, fat
21g, saturated fat 9g, fiber 4g, added sugar none, salt 1.2g

You could use cooked bacon instead of
ham, and gruyère instead of cheddar.

Florentine Egg Grill

8oz frozen leaf spinach, thawed
freshly grated nutmeg
knob of butter
2 ham slices, cut into thin strips
salt & pepper to taste
2 eggs
2 tbsp cream
3oz cheddar cheese, grated

Takes 25 minutes • Serves 2

1 Drain the thawed spinach well. Pour into a bowl
and stir in a little nutmeg, a knob of butter and the
ham. Season with salt and pepper. Form into two
mounds on the base of a shallow, buttered ovenproof dish.
2 Preheat the broiler. Poach the eggs in a pan half
full of lightly salted water until just set.
3 Lift out with a slotted spoon, drain well and place
on the spinach cakes. Drizzle with the cream and
sprinkle with the cheese. Broil until golden brown.

• Per serving: 368 calories, protein 26g, carbohydrate 3g, fat
28g, saturated fat 15g, fiber 2g, added sugar none, salt 2.12g

If you can't find fresh horseradish,
add creamed horseradish to taste. Serve with toast.

Smoked Fish and Horseradish Paté

8oz smoked fish fillets,
skinned and boned
3 tbsp freshly grated horseradish
4oz ricotta cheese
4–5 tsp fresh lemon juice
1 tsp fennel seeds, crushed
2 tbsp melted butter
bay leaves and pink or green
peppercorns, to garnish
toast or rye bread, to serve

Takes 25 minutes, plus chilling • Serves 4

1 In a food processor, blend the fish, horseradish,
ricotta, 4 teaspoons of lemon juice, fennel and
pepper to a smooth paste.
2 Taste and add more lemon juice, if necessary.
Spoon into a serving bowl and drizzle with the butter.
3 Garnish with bay leaves and peppercorns. Chill for
1 hour before serving with the toast.

• Per serving: 283 calories, protein 13g, carbohydrate 3g, fat
25g, saturated fat 9g, fiber 1g, added sugar none, salt 1.17g

A frittata is an Italian omelette. Use cheaper
smoked salmon trimmings for this light supper.

Smoked Salmon Frittata

1lb 2oz new potatoes,
thickly sliced
6oz smoked salmon
8 eggs
2 tbsp chopped fresh dill
4oz frozen baby peas
salt & pepper to taste
3 tbsp olive oil

Takes 40 minutes • Serves 4

1 Cook the potatoes in salted boiling water until just
tender, about 10 minutes. Drain and leave to cool
slightly. Cut the salmon into wide strips. Crack the
eggs into a bowl, beat with a fork until foamy, then
stir in the smoked salmon, dill and peas, and
season with salt and pepper. Finally, stir in the
potatoes.
2 Heat 3 tablespoons of olive oil in a large non-stick
frying pan and carefully pour in the egg mixture.
Cook over a fairly low heat for 10–15 minutes, until
the egg is starting to set just under the surface.
3 Put a plate over the pan and invert the frittata
onto it. Slide it back into the pan and cook 5 minutes
to brown the bottom. Slide onto a plate and cool for
5 minutes before cutting into wedges.

• Per serving: 423 calories, protein 31g, carbohydrate 22g, fat
24g, saturated fat 5g, fiber 3g, added sugar none, salt 3.15g

This spicy rice mix is a favorite
snack in Indonesia.

Nasi Goreng

12oz long grain rice
2 tbsp sunflower oil, plus 1 tsp
2 garlic cloves, roughly chopped
1lb boneless, skinless chicken
breasts or thighs, cut into chunks
1 red pepper, seeded and diced
1 tbsp curry paste or powder
bunch of scallions, thinly sliced
2 tbsp soy sauce, plus
extra to serve
2 eggs
2oz roasted peanuts,
roughly chopped
4 tbsp roughly chopped
fresh cilantro (coriander)

Takes 35 minutes • Serves 4

1 Cook the rice in salted boiling water for 12–15 minutes. Drain well. Meanwhile, heat the 2 tablespoons of oil in a wok or large frying pan.
2 Fry the garlic, chicken and pepper for 10 minutes, stirring, until golden. Add the curry paste or powder and cook for 1 minute. Stir in the rice and scallions and cook for 5 minutes, until piping hot. Stir in the 2 tablespoons of soy sauce.
3 Push the rice to one side of the wok. Pour the remaining teaspoon of oil in the space, crack in the eggs and lightly scramble them. Mix into the rice. Sprinkle on the peanuts, cilantro and extra soy sauce. Serve immediately.

• Per serving: 625 calories, protein 34g, carbohydrate 73g, fat 24g, saturated fat 2g, fiber 4g, added sugar none, salt 2.23g

Make these ahead of time and store in the refrigerator, covered with plastic wrap.

Spicy Lamb Burgers

1 onion, roughly chopped
1in piece of fresh ginger, peeled and chopped
2 garlic cloves, roughly chopped
bunch of fresh cilantro or parsley
2 tsp ground cumin
2 tsp ground coriander
1 tsp ground cinnamon
4oz dried apricots, finely chopped
1lb 9oz lean ground lamb
salt & pepper to taste
oil, for brushing

TO SERVE
6 large buns or rolls
2 tsp harissa paste (available from large supermarkets) or chili paste
8 tbsp mayonnaise
a few lettuce leaves, and tomato and cucumber slices

Takes 30 minutes • Serves 6

1 Process the onion, ginger, garlic and cilantro or parsley (stems too) in a food processor until finely chopped. Add the spices, apricots, lamb, and plenty of salt and pepper, then pulse until just mixed.

2 Shape into six burgers, brush lightly with oil and cook on a hot griddle, or under the broiler, for 4–5 minutes on each side.

3 Split and toast the buns. Swirl the harissa or chili paste into the mayonnaise. Serve the burgers with lettuce, tomato and cucumber in the buns and mayonnaise on the side.

• Per serving: 497 calories, protein 30g, carbohydrate 34g, fat 28g, saturated fat 8g, fiber 2g, added sugar none, salt 1.21g

Look for different stir fry sauces
in the supermarket, to vary this dish.

Steak and Noodle Stir Fry

8oz rump steak
8oz bok choy
1 red pepper, seeded
2 tbsp sunflower oil
2 packages instant ramen noodles

Takes 10 minutes • Serves 2

1 Cook the ramen noodles according to the directions on the package. Trim any visible fat from the steak, then slice into thin strips. Cut each head of bok choy into quarters, lengthwise. Dice the pepper into small squares.

2 Heat 2 tablespoons of sunflower oil in a wok or large frying pan. Add the pepper and stir fry quickly for 1 minute. Add the beef and stir fry until browned all over. Add the bok choy and cook briefly until it is starting to wilt.

3 Add the seasoning packets from the ramen noodles and 2 tablespoons of water and stir. Bring to a boil, then add the noodles and warm through, loosening them until they are all coated in sauce. Serve immediately.

• Per serving: 499 calories, protein 32g, carbohydrate 53.8g, fat 18.9g, saturated fat 3.1g, fiber 3.8g, added sugar 1.6g, salt 2.52g

A quick, fresh-tasting dish,
spiked with chili.

Mozzarella Pasta with Olives

2oz penne or rigatoni
1 small red onion, finely chopped
1 red chili, seeded and
finely chopped
1lb ripe tomatoes, chopped
salt & pepper to taste
6 tbsp olive oil
8oz buffalo mozzarella, chopped
handful of small, fresh basil or
mint leaves
4oz black olives

Takes 25 minutes • Serves 4

1 In a large pot of salted boiling water, cook the pasta for 10–12 minutes, stirring occasionally.
2 Meanwhile, mix together the onion, chili and tomatoes in a large bowl. Season well with salt and pepper, then stir in the olive oil.
3 Drain the pasta and add it to the tomato mixture with the mozzarella, basil and olives. Stir well and serve.

• Per serving: 650 calories, protein 24g, carbohydrate 71g, fat 32g, saturated fat 10g, fiber 5g, added sugar none, salt 2.26g

These tiny tomatoes taste extra sweet when roasted,
and are a contrast to the salty cheese.

Spaghetti with Cherry Tomatoes

1lb 2oz cherry tomatoes
3 tbsp olive oil
salt & pepper to taste
14oz spaghetti
9oz feta cheese
generous handful fresh flatleaf
parsley
handful of black olives
freshly grated parmesan cheese,
to serve

Takes 25 minutes • Serves 4

1 Preheat the oven to 400°F. Put the tomatoes into a shallow ovenproof dish, drizzle with 3 tablespoons of olive oil, and season with salt and pepper. Roast for 15 minutes until slightly scorched.
2 Cook the spaghetti in plenty of salted boiling water for 10–12 minutes, until just tender. Meanwhile, cut the feta into cubes and roughly chop the parsley.
3 Drain the pasta, then return to the pot. Add the roasted tomatoes, along with their pan juices, the feta, olives and parsley. Toss together until well mixed, then serve with freshly grated parmesan.

• Per serving: 530 calories, protein 23g, carbohydrate 79g, fat 16g, saturated fat 8g, fiber 5g, added sugar none, salt 3.02g

A creamy vegetarian pasta that's perfect when
you're in the mood for some comfort food.

Penne with Blue Cheese

12oz penne
8oz frozen leaf spinach
3oz Danish blue cheese, crumbled
pinch of chili pepper flakes
black pepper
8oz mascarpone cheese
1oz freshly grated parmesan cheese
mixed salad greens, to serve

Takes 20 minutes • Serves 4

1 Bring a large pot of salted water to a boil. Add the pasta and cook for 10–12 minutes, until tender, adding the spinach to the pan for the last 3 minutes of cooking time. Drain.
2 Put the pasta and spinach into a shallow heat-proof dish, along with the blue cheese, chili flakes and plenty of black pepper.
3 Dot spoonfuls of the mascarpone over the top of the pasta mixture. Sprinkle with the parmesan and broil for 5 minutes, until the mascarpone melts into a sauce and the parmesan turns golden. Serve with a green salad.

• Per serving: 698 calories, protein 21g, carbohydrate 70g, fat 39g, saturated fat 24g, fiber 4g, added sugar none, salt 1.06g

Mushrooms add a deliciously nutty flavor
and juicy texture to this vegetarian pasta dish.

Tagliatelle with Goat's Cheese

9oz mushrooms
1 small onion
2 garlic cloves
6oz tagliatelle
1oz butter
1 tbsp olive oil, plus
extra for drizzling
4oz firm goat's cheese
black pepper
freshly shaved parmesan cheese,
to serve

Takes 20 minutes • Serves 2
(easily doubled)

1 Slice the mushrooms and finely chop the onion and garlic. Cook the pasta in plenty of salted boiling water, according to the package instructions.
2 Heat the butter and oil in a frying pan until the butter is melted. Add the onion and cook until golden, about 3–4 minutes. Stir in the garlic and mushrooms and cook, stirring, until the mushrooms are golden brown.
3 Drain the pasta, reserving 4 tablespoons of the pasta water. Return the pasta to its pot with the reserved water and stir in the mushroom mixture. Roughly break the goat's cheese into pieces and gently stir it into the pasta so it starts to melt. Serve sprinkled with black pepper, a drizzle of olive oil and a few shavings of parmesan.

• Per serving: 598 calories, protein 20g, carbohydrate 71g, fat 28g, saturated fat 8g, fiber 5g, added sugar none, salt 0.88g

Tubular pasta shapes work best in this recipe, because the sauce gets trapped inside and clings to their ridged surfaces.

Stilton and Broccoli Pasta

12oz penne or rigatoni
12oz broccoli, cut into florets
5oz stilton cheese
(or blue cheese or gorgonzola)
6 thick slices bacon
6oz crème fraîche (or cream mixed with 1/2 tsp buttermilk)
black pepper

Takes 25 minutes • Serves 4

1 Cook the pasta in a large pot of salted boiling water for 5 minutes. Add the broccoli, return the water to a boil and cook 5–7 minutes more, until the pasta and broccoli are just tender.
2 While the pasta is cooking, crumble the stilton into a small bowl. Cook the bacon until crispy, then cut into pieces. Drain the pasta, reserving a few tablespoons of the cooking water. Return the pasta and reserved water to the pot.
3 Stir in the crumbled stilton, crème fraîche and plenty of freshly ground black pepper. Stir gently until the cheese starts to melt into the sauce. Serve sprinkled with the bacon pieces and freshly ground black pepper.

• Per serving: 736 calories, protein 30g, carbohydrate 70g, fat 39g, saturated fat 20g, fiber 5g, added sugar none, salt 2.2g

You'll find most of these ingredients in your pantry.
Vary the green vegetables as you like.

Broccoli and Spaghetti Bake

1 tbsp olive oil
1 onion, chopped
15oz can chopped tomatoes
salt & pepper to taste
1oz butter
1oz all-purpose flour
2 cups 2% milk
ground nutmeg to taste
10oz broken-up spaghetti
10oz broccoli, cut into florets
4oz sharp cheddar cheese, grated

Takes 45 minutes • Serves 4

1 Heat the oil in a small pan and saute the onion until soft. Stir in the tomatoes and season with salt and pepper. Boil for 10 minutes, stirring until thickened. Meanwhile, put the butter, flour and milk into a saucepan. Season with a little nutmeg. Bring to a boil, whisking until thick and smooth.
2 Cook the spaghetti in salted boiling water for 8 minutes, then add the broccoli and cook 4 more minutes. Preheat the broiler. Stir most of the cheese into the white sauce.
3 Drain the pasta, mix with the cheese sauce and spoon half into a 2-quart baking dish. Spoon the tomato sauce on top of the paster. Cover with the rest of the pasta and sprinkle with the remaining cheese. Broil for 5–8 minutes, until golden.

• Per serving: 574 calories, protein 26g, carbohydrate 75g, fat 21g, saturated fat 11g, fiber 6g, added sugar none, salt 0.98g

Salty anchovies and capers add a piquant
flavor to peppery watercress sauce.

Linguine with Watercress Sauce

10oz linguine or spaghetti
1 garlic clove, peeled
6 anchovies in oil, drained
1 tbsp capers, drained and
rinsed well
2oz watercress
6 tbsp olive oil
salt & pepper to taste

Takes 20 minutes • Serves 4

1 Cook the pasta in a large pot of salted boiling water, according to the package instructions, until tender.

2 Meanwhile, put the garlic, anchovies and capers in a food processor and process until well blended. Add the watercress and process again until the mixture is finely chopped. With the motor running, drizzle in the olive oil to make a soft paste.

3 Mix 4 tablespoons of the pasta cooking water into the watercress sauce, then season with salt and pepper. Drain the pasta and return to the pot. Stir in the sauce and divide among four bowls. Grind plenty of black pepper over the top and serve immediately.

• Per serving: 422 calories, protein 11g, carbohydrate 56g, fat 19g, saturated fat 3g, fiber 3g, added sugar none, salt 0.53g

Reduce the calories by using a
low-fat soft cheese with garlic and herbs.

Creamy Salmon Pasta

10oz penne or rigatoni
12oz broccoli, cut into small florets
10oz boneless, skinless salmon
(about 2 fillets)
salt & pepper to taste
5oz soft cheese with
garlic and herbs
5oz cream
2 tbsp sundried tomato paste

Takes 20 minutes • Serves 4

1 Cook the pasta according to the package instructions, adding the broccoli for the last 3 minutes of cooking. Meanwhile, put the salmon in a frying pan, season with salt and pepper and just cover with water. Bring to a boil, then simmer, covered, for 6 minutes until the flesh flakes easily with a fork. Using a slotted spoon, transfer to a plate and keep warm.

2 Mix the soft cheese with the cream and sundried tomato paste to make a smooth sauce. Season to taste with salt and pepper.

3 Drain the pasta and broccoli, then return to the pot. Pour in the sauce and stir well. Flake the salmon into large chunks and gently mix into the pasta. Transfer to a warm serving bowl, season with black pepper and serve.

• Per serving: 586 calories, protein 33g, carbohydrate 61g, fat 25g, saturated fat 6g, fiber 5g, added sugar none, salt 0.53g

Try this easy, no-cook sauce when
you see crab meat on sale.

Tagliatelle with Crab and Salsa

8oz tagliatelle
4 tbsp olive oil
1 tbsp fresh lemon juice
salt and pepper to taste
3 tbsp chopped fresh parsley
1 small red onion, finely chopped
3 ripe tomatoes, seeded
and chopped
6oz canned crab meat, drained, or
fresh or frozen crab
mixed salad greens, to serve

Takes 20 minutes • Serves 2

1 Cook the tagliatelle in a large pot of salted boiling water for 10–12 minutes, or according to the package instructions.
2 Whisk together the olive oil and lemon juice, season with salt and pepper, and stir in the parsley.
3 Drain the pasta and toss with the olive oil mixture, red onion, tomatoes and crab meat. Serve immediately with a green salad.

• Per serving: 634 calories, protein 26g, carbohydrate 82g, fat 25g, saturated fat 3g, fiber 5g, added sugar none, salt 1.02g

Use fresh raw shrimp for special occasions,
but frozen ones will do for a midweek supper.

Shrimp Tagliatelle with Lemon

12oz tagliatelle
8oz green beans,
trimmed and cut in half
3oz butter
2 tbsp olive oil
finely grated zest and juice of
1 small lemon
10oz raw peeled large shrimp
salt & pepper to taste
2 tbsp chopped fresh dill, to serve

Takes 15 minutes • Serves 4

1 Cook the pasta according to the package instructions. Three minutes before the end of the cooking time, throw in the green beans.

2 While the pasta is cooking, melt the butter in a pan and stir in the olive oil, lemon zest and juice, and the shrimp. Cook over low heat for 3–4 minutes, stirring occasionally, until the shrimp turns pink. Season with salt and pepper.

3 Drain the pasta and beans, reserving about 4 tablespoons of the cooking liquid. Toss with the shrimp and add enough cooking liquid to make a sauce. Serve sprinkled with the fresh dill.

• Per serving: 581 calories, protein 25g, carbohydrate 68g, fat 25g, saturated fat 12g, fiber 4g, added sugar none, salt 0.79g

Try adding shrimp instead of bacon,
and chopped fresh dill instead of parsley.

Pasta and Cod Bake

12oz pasta shells
6 thick bacon slices,
cut into strips
12oz of your favorite tomato
sauce
finely grated zest of 1 lemon
1lb 2oz cod fillets, cut
into 1½in pieces
4 tbsp crème fraîche (or half-and-
half mixed with 1/2 tsp buttermilk)
3 tbsp chopped fresh parsley
salt & pepper to taste
2oz freshly grated cheddar
or parmesan cheese

Takes 25 minutes • Serves 4

1 Cook the pasta in salted boiling water for 10–12 minutes until tender, stirring once.
2 Cook the bacon for 5 minutes, until crisp. Add the tomato sauce and stir well until it just starts to bubble. Stir in the lemon zest and add the cod. Cover and cook for 4 minutes, until the fish is just cooked.
3 Preheat the broiler. Drain the pasta and stir into the sauce with the crème fraîche and parsley. Season with salt and pepper. Spoon into a shallow heatproof dish. Sprinkle the cheese on top and broil until it is melted and golden.

• Per serving: 651 calories, protein 44g, carbohydrate 72g, fat 23g, saturated fat 10g, fiber 4g, added sugar 2g, salt 3.24g

This all-in-one sauce gives perfect results.
Whisk until the mixture boils, then simmer for 5 minutes.

Pasta and Haddock Gratin

12oz penne or rigatoni
6oz frozen leaf spinach
1oz butter
1oz all-purpose flour
2 cups milk
1lb skinless haddock or cod
fillets, cut into chunks
16oz sharp cheddar cheese, grated
salt & pepper to taste
2 tomatoes, sliced

Takes 30 minutes • Serves 4

1 Cook the pasta in salted boiling water for about 12 minutes. Add the spinach for the last 3 minutes of cooking time.

2 Meanwhile, whisk the butter, flour and milk in a large pan until the mixture comes to a boil. Reduce the heat, add the fish and simmer for 5 minutes, or until the fish is just cooked. Remove from the heat and stir in three-quarters of the cheese. Season with salt and pepper.

3 Preheat the broiler. Drain the pasta and stir into the sauce. Pour into a 1-quart shallow ovenproof dish. Put the tomatoes on top and sprinkle with the remaining cheese. Broil for 5–7 minutes, until golden.

• Per serving: 751 calories, protein 48g, carbohydrate 80g, fat 29g, saturated fat 17g, fiber 4g, added sugar none, salt 1.61g

You can substitute walnuts in this dish, if pine nuts are difficult to find in the supermarket.

Spinach, Bacon and Pine Nut Pasta

finely grated zest of 1 lemon,
plus 2 tbsp lemon juice
3 tbsp olive oil, plus extra
for drizzling
salt & pepper to taste
10oz pasta, such as pappardelle
4 slices bacon, cut into strips
2oz pine nuts
8oz baby leaf spinach,
thick stalks removed

Takes 25 minutes • Serves 4
(easily halved)

1 Mix the lemon zest and juice with the olive oil. Season with salt and pepper and set aside. Cook the pasta in a large pot of salted boiling water for 10–12 minutes.

2 Meanwhile, cook the bacon until crisp. Pout off most of the bacon fat, then add the pine nuts and cook with the bacon until the nuts are toasted golden.

3 Drain the pasta, return to the hot pot and add the spinach leaves, stirring gently until wilted. Toss in the bacon, pine nuts and lemon dressing. Season to taste, then serve drizzled with a little olive oil and sprinkled with black pepper.

• Per serving: 495 calories, protein 16g, carbohydrate 59g, fat 23g, saturated fat 4g, fiber 4g, added sugar none, salt 0.86g

Instead of a sauce, this light, summery pasta
has a mustard vinaigrette dressing.

Pasta with Asparagus and Mustard

9oz spaghetti
10oz thick sliced bacon
9oz asparagus, cut into 1in pieces
9oz cherry tomatoes, halved
2oz parmesan cheese shavings
(use a potato peeler)

FOR THE DRESSING
5 tbsp olive oil
1½ tbsp white wine vinegar
2 tsp Dijon mustard
salt & pepper to taste

Takes 25 minutes • Serves 4

1 To make the dressing, put all the ingredients in a bowl and whisk until creamy. Season with salt and pepper, then set aside. Break the spaghetti into 3-inch pieces and cook in salted boiling water for 10–12 minutes, until just tender.
2 Cut the bacon into strips and cook for 5–6 minutes. Drain all but 1 tablespoon of the fat. Add the asparagus and saute for 3–4 minutes. Add the tomatoes and cook for 2 minutes.
3 Drain the pasta and place in a serving bowl. Mix in the bacon and asparagus mixture and the mustard dressing. Top with parmesan shavings. Serve warm or cold with extra black pepper.

• Per serving: 610 calories, protein 27g, carbohydrate 50g, fat 35g, saturated fat 10g, fiber 4g, added sugar none, salt 3.5g

Tzatziki, a cucumber and mint dip from Greece,
adds a refreshing kick to this dish.

Summer Garden Spaghetti

8oz slab bacon, chopped
12oz spaghetti
9oz green beans, sliced diagonally
9oz cherry tomatoes, halved
6oz tzatziki, or plain yogurt mixed
with chopped mint leaves
black pepper

Takes 25 minutes • Serves 4
(easily halved)

1 Cook the bacon until crisp. Drain on paper towels.
2 Meanwhile, bring a large pot of salted water to a boil, add the spaghetti, stir once and cook at a rolling boil for 6 minutes. Stir in the beans and cook for 6 minutes, more until tender.
3 Drain the pasta and beans and return to the pot. Add the bacon and cooking juices, the tomatoes and tzatziki. Toss together well, and season with plenty of black pepper. Serve warm.

• Per serving: 515 calories, protein 22g, carbohydrate 70g, fat 19g, saturated fat 7g, fiber 5g, added sugar 5g, salt 2.02g

If you can't find orecchiette pasta (literally "little ears," so-called because of their curved shape), substitute another shape.

Pasta with Bacon and Peas

10oz pasta shapes, such as orecchiette
8oz frozen peas
1 tbsp olive oil
1 onion, chopped
4 thick slices bacon, cut into strips
3½fl oz crème fraîche (or half-and-half mixed with 1/2 tsp buttermilk)
salt & pepper to taste
fresh country bread and mixed salad greens, to serve

Takes 20 minutes • Serves 4

1 Cook the pasta in salted boiling water for 12 minutes, adding the frozen peas for the last 3 minutes of cooking.

2 Meanwhile, heat the oil in a frying pan, then cook the onion for 2–3 minutes until it is starting to brown. Add the bacon and cook over a high heat, stirring, until both the bacon and onion are golden and crisp.

3 Drain the pasta and toss with the onion and bacon. Stir in the crème fraîche. Season with salt and pepper. Serve piping hot with fresh country bread and a simple green salad.

• Per serving: 461 calories, protein 17g, carbohydrate 65g, fat 17g, saturated fat 7g, fiber 5g, added sugar none, salt 1.07g

You can get very creative with the vegetables in this dish, substituting almost anything for the zucchini.

Ham and Zucchini Tagliatelle

14oz dried tagliatelle
3 tbsp olive oil
1 plump garlic clove, halved and thinly sliced
4 zucchini, very thinly sliced
6oz thinly sliced ham, cut into thin strips
3 tbsp pesto
salt & pepper to taste

Takes 25 minutes • Serves 4

1 Cook the tagliatelle in salted boiling water for 8–10 minutes, until just tender.
2 Meanwhile, heat the oil in a large pan or wok. Add the garlic slices and the zucchini, and stir fry over high heat for about 3 minutes until soft and lightly browned. (You may need to do this in two batches.) Add the ham and toss until heated through.
3 Drain the pasta well, add to the zucchini with the pesto, and season to taste with salt and pepper. Toss well and serve.

• Per serving: 555 calories, protein 24g, carbohydrate 77g, fat 19g, saturated fat 5g, fiber 4g, added sugar none, salt 1.31g

Using ready-made sauce saves time and effort. Look for
fresh sauces in the refrigerated section of your supermarket.

Fusilli with Turkey and Mushrooms

1 tbsp olive oil
1 onion, sliced
1 red pepper, seeded and chopped
1lb boneless turkey, cut into chunks
12oz fusilli
10–12oz your favorite mushroom
sauce
2 cups milk milk
8oz ham, cut into chunks
8oz frozen leaf spinach
salt & pepper to taste
freshly grated nutmeg
4oz sharp cheddar cheese, grated

Takes 25 minutes • Serves 6

1 Heat the oil in a large pan, then saute the onion and pepper for 5 minutes. Add the turkey and cook for another 5 minutes, stirring occasionally. Cook the pasta in a pot of salted boiling water for about 8–10 minutes, until just tender. Drain well.
2 Preheat the broiler. Mix the milk into the mushroom sauce. Add the mushroom sauce mix to the turkey in the pan and bring to a boil, then stir in the pasta, ham and frozen spinach.
3 Season with salt and pepper, and add nutmeg to taste. Simmer for 5 minutes, until very hot. Spoon into a shallow heatproof dish, sprinkle with the cheese, and broil until brown.

• Per serving: 501 calories, protein 40g, carbohydrate 51g, fat 17g, saturated fat 7g, fiber 3g, added sugar none, salt 2.54g

Tuna and bacon may seem an odd
combination, but they taste good together.

Stir-fried Tuna Rice

12oz long grain rice
8 thick slices bacon, roughly chopped
2 tbsp vegetable oil
8oz frozen peas, thawed
6oz tuna, drained
2–3 tbsp soy sauce, plus extra to serve

Takes 30 minutes • Serves 4

1 Cook the rice, following the instructions on the package, then set aside to cool slightly.
2 Heat a wok until hot. Add the bacon and stir fry for 2 minutes until crispy and browned. Remove from the wok and set aside.
3 Heat the oil in the wok and stir fry the rice for 2 minutes. Add the peas and tuna and stir fry over high heat for 2–3 minutes. Add the soy sauce and crispy bacon and cook for 1 minute more. Serve immediately, with extra soy sauce, if you like.

• Per serving: 552 calories, protein 25g, carbohydrate 81g, fat 17g, saturated fat 5g, fiber 3g, added sugar none, salt 2.98g

Spanish chorizo sausages are perfect for this dish, or use one of the many brands of spicy sausages in supermarket.

Spicy Sausage Rice

2 tbsp olive oil
4 spicy sausages, sliced
1 onion, sliced
10oz arborio rice
5oz sundried tomato pesto or
pasta sauce
3½ cups vegetable stock
salt & pepper to taste

Takes 30 minutes • Serves 4

1 Heat the oil in a heavy pot, then fry the sausages for 10 minutes until cooked through. Remove from the pot. Add the onion and cook at low heat for 7 minutes, stirring often, until softened. Stir in the rice and cook for 2 minutes, until the grains glisten.

2 Add the pasta sauce and stock, stir and bring to a boil. Reduce the heat and simmer, covered, for 12–15 minutes, stirring occasionally, until the rice has a creamy texture.

3 Stir the sausages into the rice. Remove from the heat and season with black pepper. Sprinkle with salt, if necessary, then stir and serve.

• Per serving: 488 calories, protein 16g, carbohydrate 69g, fat 19g, saturated fat 5g, fiber 2g, added sugar 2g, salt 2.32g

No crackers? Crush a large handful of cornflakes
to make an equally quick and simple coating.

Parmesan Chicken

4 boneless, skinless chicken breasts
juice of 1 small lemon
salt & pepper to taste
1 egg
4 saltine crackers
2oz parmesan cheese, finely grated
2 tbsp oil
4 tbsp sour cream
4 tsp mild chili oil or sauce
mixed salad and new potatoes,
to serve

Takes 30 minutes • Serves 4

1 Cut each chicken breast into quarters and season
with lemon juice, salt and pepper. Beat the egg and
pour into a shallow bowl. Put the crackers in a bag
and crush into crumbs, then mix with the parmesan
on a small plate.
2 Dip the chicken in the egg,, then the cracker
mixture, pressing it on evenly. Heat the oil in a large
pan and cook the chicken 4–5 minutes on each
side, until it is well browned, crisp and cooked
through.
3 Transfer the chicken to serving plates, spoon
some sour cream onto each plate and drizzle over
the chili oil. Serve with a crisp salad and new
potatoes.

• Per serving: 345 calories, protein 32g, carbohydrate 7g, fat
21g, saturated fat 9g, fiber trace, added sugar none, salt 0.78g

Cook potato wedges, tossed in oil, on a baking sheet
in the oven, on the rack above the chicken.

Crunchy Almond Chicken

4 boneless, skinless chicken
breasts, 5oz each
4oz stilton or other blue-veined
cheese, crumbled
olive oil, for brushing
salt & pepper to taste
2oz almonds, chopped
2 tbsp chopped fresh parsley
4 tbsp cranberry sauce
frozen potato wedges, to serve

Takes 50 minutes • Serves 4

1 Preheat the oven to 375°F. Slit a pocket in each
chicken breast and stuff with the cheese. Put in a
shallow ovenproof dish, brush lightly with oil and
season with salt and pepper.
2 Mix the nuts and parsley, then press onto the
chicken and bake, uncovered, for 25 minutes until
golden and cooked through.
3 Gently heat the cranberry sauce in a small pan.
Serve the chicken with the sauce and potatoes.

• Per serving: 400 calories, protein 39g, carbohydrate 15g, fat
21g, saturated fat 8g, fiber 1g, added sugar 14g, salt 1.11g

Made from just five ingredients, but fancy enough
to serve to company.

Chicken Rarebits

4 skinless, boneless chicken breasts
olive oil, for greasing
5oz cheddar cheese, coarsely grated
1 rounded tbsp wholegrain mustard
3 tbsp whole milk
5oz cherry tomatoes
broccoli and new potatoes, to serve

Takes 35 minutes • Serves 4

1 Preheat the oven to 400ºF. Slice the breasts in half horizontally, so you have two thinner pieces that will cook more quickly. Lightly oil a shallow baking dish and arrange the chicken in a single layer. Mix the cheese, mustard and milk, and pile the mixture on top of each piece of chicken.

2 Arrange the tomatoes all around the chicken, then cook for 20–30 minutes, until the chicken is golden and the tomatoes squishy.

3 Serve with broccoli and new potatoes. Suggest to everyone that they squash the tomatoes on their plates to blend into the cheesy sauce.

• Per serving: 316 calories, protein 44g, carbohydrate 2g, fat 15g, saturated fat 8g, fiber 1g, added sugar none, salt 1.09g

Chicken thighs are cheap but tasty,
especially in this chunky ratatouille-like sauce.

Spicy Tomato Chicken

2 tbsp seasoned flour
½–1 tsp chili powder
8 chicken thighs
1 tbsp vegetable oil
1 onion, chopped
2 cups chicken stock
2 garlic cloves, chopped
2 tbsp tomato paste
2 zucchini, cut into chunks
1lb tomatoes, quartered
mashed potatoes, to serve

Takes 50 minutes • Serves 4

1 Mix together the seasoned flour and chili powder. Use to coat the chicken thighs. Set aside the remaining seasoned flour. Heat the oil in a large frying pan with a lid. Add the chicken and cook over a moderately high heat for 8–10 minutes, turning once, until browned all over. Transfer to a plate.
2 Add the onion to the pan and cook for 5–6 minutes, stirring occasionally, until softened. Sprinkle in the reserved seasoned flour and cook for 1 minute, stirring continuously. Stir in the stock, garlic and tomato paste.
3 Return the chicken to the pan and bring to a boil. Scatter the zucchini and tomatoes around the pan, mix, cover and simmer for 15–20 minutes. Serve with mashed potatoes.

• Per serving: 424 calories, protein 33g, carbohydrate 19g, fat 25g, saturated fat 7g, fiber 3g, added sugar none, salt 1.2g

All the flavors of the Sunday roast, but easy enough for a midweek meal.

Baked Chicken with Stuffing Balls

8 chicken thighs
4 carrots, cut into chunks
1 tbsp fresh rosemary or 2 tsp dried
2 tbsp oil
4 potatoes, cut into wedges
1 tbsp all-purpose flour
1½ cups chicken stock
1 tsp tomato paste

FOR THE STUFFING
1 large onion, chopped
1oz butter
8oz fresh white breadcrumbs
finely grated zest of 1 lemon
2 tsp dried thyme
2 tbsp chopped fresh parsley
1 egg, beaten
salt & pepper to taste

Takes 1 hour 40 minutes • Serves 4

1 Preheat the oven to 400°F. Put the chicken and carrots in a roasting pan and sprinkle with the rosemary and half the oil. Put the potatoes in a smaller pan and toss in the remaining oil. Bake the chicken and potatoes for 10 minutes.

2 To make the stuffing, saute the onion in the butter for 5 minutes. Mix in the breadcrumbs, lemon zest, thyme, parsley and egg. Season with salt and pepper. Shape into eight balls and arrange among the chicken and carrots after they have cooked 10 minutes. Bake everything for 1 hour, until cooked and golden.

3 Remove everything from the pans and keep warm. Pour off the fat from the chicken pan, leaving the juices. Stir in the flour and cook for 2 minutes on the stove until golden. Add the stock and tomato paste, stirring all the time, until thickened. Serve with the chicken and vegetables.

• Per serving: 645 calories, protein 50g, carbohydrate 73g, fat 19g, saturated fat 6g, fiber 6g, added sugar none, salt 2.77g

Use ready-made sauce and pastry to save
time on the preparation of this tasty pie.

Easy Chicken and Spinach Pie

2 tbsp olive oil
4 boneless, skinless chicken thigh
fillets, cut into 1in chunks
8oz button mushrooms, halved
9oz frozen loose-leaf spinach
8oz your favorite porcini
mushroom sauce
salt & pepper to taste
14oz ready-made puff pastry
beaten egg, for glazing

Takes 50 minutes • Serves 4

1 Preheat the oven to 425°F. Heat the oil in a frying pan and cook the chicken, stirring occasionally, for 10 minutes until browned. Add the mushrooms and cook 2 minutes more. Stir in the spinach and the mushroom sauce and season with salt and pepper.
2 Spoon into a 9-inch quiche pan or pie dish. Brush the rim of the dish with water and lay the sheet of pastry over the filling. Press on to the rim to seal, then trim the pastry edges.
3 Brush the top with beaten egg and make a small air vent in the middle of the pastry lid with the tip of a knife. Bake for 30–35 minutes, until the pastry is crisp, puffed up and golden brown.

• Per serving: 603 calories, protein 30g, carbohydrate 41g, fat 36g, saturated fat 3g, fiber 2g, added sugar none, salt 1.36g

Get the rice cooking before you start to stir fry.
This recipe also works well with beef or chicken.

Lamb and Scallion Stir Fry

3 tbsp soy sauce
3 tbsp sherry
3 tbsp sesame oil
2 tsp wine vinegar
2 garlic cloves
bunch of scallions
1lb boneless lamb
3 tbsp vegetable oil
cooked rice, to serve

Takes 20 minutes • Serves 4
(easily halved)

1 In a bowl, mix together the soy sauce, sherry, sesame oil and vinegar with 4 tablespoons of water. Slice the garlic thinly. Cut the scallions, including the green parts, into 2-inch lengths, using a diagonal cut. Slice the lamb thinly across the grain.
2 Heat the oil in a large frying pan or wok, then add the garlic and stir briefly. Add the lamb and stir fry for 1–2 minutes, until browned.
3 Stir in the soy sauce mixture and let bubble briefly. Add the scallions and cook for a few seconds, until they just start to soften. Serve with the rice.

• Per serving: 435 calories, protein 22g, carbohydrate 2g, fat 36g, saturated fat 12g, fiber 1g, added sugar none, salt 2.21g

Use boneless lamb from the leg to be sure the meat is tender.
Marinate the pieces the day before cooking.

Chili Lamb Skewers

1lb 9oz lean, boneless lamb
small bunch of mint, stalks removed
1 fresh red chili, seeded
3 tbsp olive oil
salt & pepper to taste
2 small red onions
5oz low-fat plain yogurt
mixed salad greens and
new potatoes, to serve

Takes 30 minutes • Serves 4

1 Cut the lamb into bite-size chunks. Chop the mint and put half in a large bowl and half in a small bowl. Finely chop the chili and add half to each bowl.
2 Stir 3 tablespoons of olive oil into the large bowl, season with salt and pepper, then add the lamb and turn until it is glistening and well coated. Finely chop half an onion and add to the small bowl with the yogurt. Season, stir well, then cover and chill until ready to eat (it will keep for a day in the refrigerator). Cut the rest of the onion into wedges and separate the layers.
3 Thread the lamb on to four large skewers (if the skewers wooden, soak them in water first to prevent burning), with pieces of onion in between. Preheat the barbecue or broiler and cook the skewers for 6–8 minutes, turning until they are evenly browned. Serve with the yogurt, a salad and potatoes.

• Per serving: 307 calories, protein 38g, carbohydrate 6g, fat 15g, saturated fat 7g, fiber none, added sugar none, salt 0.39g

Roughly mashed root vegetables make a colorful accompaniment to roast meat, sausages or chops.

Lamb with Root Vegetable Mash

2 parsnips, peeled and cubed
1 small swede or 3 carrots,
peeled and cubed
1lb 5oz starchy potatoes
8 lamb chops (or 4 pork chops)
olive oil, for brushing
2 tsp dried rosemary
salt & pepper to taste
5oz sour cream
2 tsp wholegrain mustard

Takes 40 minutes • Serves 4

1 Cook all the vegetables in a large pot of salted boiling water for 15–18 minutes, until tender. Preheat the broiler.
2 Brush the chops with a little oil, sprinkle with rosemary and season with salt and pepper. Broil the chops for 4–5 minutes on each side.
3 Drain the vegetables and mash with a fork, then stir in the sour cream and mustard and season well. Serve with the lamb.

• Per serving: 541 calories, protein 47g, carbohydrate 41g, fat 22g, saturated fat 11g, fiber 7g, added sugar none, salt 0.46g

A one-pot meal—all you need to serve with
it is a green vegetable.

Greek Lamb with Potatoes

1lb 10oz boneless lamb fillets,
or 8 chops
salt & pepper to taste
2 tsp dried oregano
2lb 4oz starchy potatoes, sliced
2 onions, sliced
3 tbsp olive oil
4 large garlic cloves
1 cup meat or chicken
stock, or water

Takes 1¼ hours • Serves 4

1 Preheat the oven to 375°F. Dry the meat with a paper towel and sprinkle with salt, pepper and half the oregano.
2 Put the potatoes and onions in a roasting pan and drizzle with 3 tablespoons of olive oil and the rest of the oregano. Season with salt and pepper.
Mix until the potatoes and onions are well coated.
Tuck the unpeeled garlic cloves among the potatoes.
3 Roast the potatoes for 20 minutes until they are just starting to soften, then put the meat on top.
Pour in the stock or water and return to the oven for 30–35 minutes, until the lamb is tender and the potatoes are just starting to brown. Make sure everyone gets a roasted garlic clove to squeeze out and mix with the other ingredients.

• Per serving: 545 calories, protein 44g, carbohydrate 50g, fat 20g, saturated fat 9g, fiber 4g, added sugar none, salt 0.61g

If you can't find an assortment of mushrooms in the vegetable aisle of the supermarket, see what's available in cans.

Liver with Mixed Mushrooms

10oz liver, sliced
2 tbsp seasoned flour
2 tbsp oil
5oz mixed mushrooms
2 garlic cloves, finely chopped
1 cup chicken stock
good handful chopped fresh parsley
mashed potatoes, to serve

Takes 15 minutes • Serves 2

1 Coat the slices of liver in the seasoned flour. Heat 1 tablespoon of the oil in a frying pan. Add the liver and cook for 30 seconds on each side until just browned. Remove from the pan and set aside.

2 Pour the remaining 1 tablespoon of oil into the pan and saute the mushrooms and garlic for 2–3 minutes. Pour in the stock and return the liver to the pan. Simmer for 1–2 minutes.

3 Stir in the parsley and season. Serve with mashed potatoes.

• Per serving: 390 calories, protein 35g, carbohydrate 17g, fat 21g, saturated fat 4g, fiber 1g, added sugar none, salt 1.17g

Liven up a simple pork cutlet by dipping it in lemon
juice, then coating with a mixture of breadcrumbs and herbs.

Lemon and Oregano Pork

finely grated zest and juice
of 1 lemon
4oz plain breadcrumbs
2 tsp dried oregano
4 pork cutlets, pounded thin
2 tbsp sunflower oil
lemon mayonnaise, potatoes and
green beans, to serve

Takes 20 minutes • Serves 4

1 On a plate, mix together the lemon zest,
breadcrumbs and oregano. Pour the lemon juice on
to another plate. Dip each pork cutlet first in the
lemon juice and then into the breadcrumb mixture
until well coated.
2 Heat the oil in a large frying pan over a high heat
and cook the pork for 3–4 minutes on each side,
until the crumbs are crisp and the pork is cooked
through.
3 Serve each cutlet with a spoonful of lemon
mayonnaise, some potatoes and green beans.

• Per serving: 291 calories, protein 29g, carbohydrate 20g, fat
11g, saturated fat 2g, fiber 1g, added sugar none, salt 0.68g

Make a more sophisticated sauce for the pork by replacing half the stock with white wine.

Speedy Pork Pan Fry

1lb 2oz boneless pork tenderloin
1 tbsp all-purpose flour
2 tsp dried rosemary
3 tbsp olive oil
9oz mushrooms, sliced
1 large garlic clove, finely chopped
1 cup vegetable stock
rice or mashed potatoes,
and vegetables, to serve

Takes 20 minutes • Serves 4

1 Cut the pork diagonally into finger-thick slices. Put the flour and rosemary in a plastic bag, season and add the pork. Toss until the meat is well coated.

2 Heat 2 tablespoons of the oil in a large frying pan. Add the pork and cook for about 3–4 minutes, turning once, until browned on both sides. Remove from the pan.

3 Heat the remaining oil in the pan and saute the mushrooms until they soften, about 2 minutes. Add the garlic and return the pork to the pan with any flour left in the bag. Gradually stir in the stock and bring to a boil. Simmer for 5 minutes, or until the pork is cooked through. Serve with rice or mashed potatoes, and vegetables.

• Per serving: 288 calories, protein 30g, carbohydrate 5g, fat 17g, saturated fat 4g, fiber 1g, added sugar none, salt 0.42g

If you can't get these thin meat slices, buy boneless pork fillets. Put between plastic wrap and flatten by pounding with a rolling pin.

Creamy Pork Escalopes

4 tsp all-purpose flour
1 tsp dried sage
4 pork escalopes
2 tbsp oil
knob of butter
1 small onion, finely chopped
8oz mushrooms, sliced
3 tbsp sherry
7oz crème fraîche (or cream mixed with 1/2 tsp buttermilk)
noodles, to serve

Takes 30 minutes • Serves 4
(easily halved)

1 Mix the flour with the sage, season, and use to coat the escalopes. Heat 1 tablespoon of the oil and the butter in a frying pan and cook the pork quickly on each side until nicely browned. Remove from the pan and keep warm.

2 Heat the remaining oil and saute the onion for 1 minute. Add the mushrooms and saute for 2–3 minutes. Add the sherry and let the mixture bubble, scraping up any bits with a wooden spoon.

3 Stir in the crème fraîche. Add the pork and heat through gently for 5 minutes. Serve with noodles.

• Per serving: 437 calories, protein 28g, carbohydrate 9g, fat 31g, saturated fat 13g, fiber 1g, added sugar none, salt 0.34g

A simple dish enriched with caramelized
onions and sour cream.

Paprika Pork

2 tbsp olive oil
3 onions, thinly sliced
1lb 5oz boneless pork
2 tbsp paprika
1 cup chicken or vegetable stock
4 oz sour cream
freshly chopped parsley, to garnish
rice and a green vegetable, to serve

Takes 55 minutes • Serves 4

1 Heat 2 tablespoons oil in a pan, add the onions
and saute on low heat for 10–15 minutes, stirring
occasionally, until softened and lightly colored.
2 Cut the pork into bite-size pieces, add to the pan
and stir over a fairly high heat to sear and brown all
over. Stir in the paprika, cook briefly, then add the
stock and bring to a boil.
3 Lower the heat, cover and cook for 30–35 minutes, until the pork is tender. Stir in the sour cream
and simmer 2 minutes more. Sprinkle the parsley
over the pork, then serve with rice and a green
vegetable.

• Per serving: 357 calories, protein 36.5g, carbohydrate 11.3g,
fat 18.7g, saturated fat 7.6g, fiber 1.3g, added sugar none, salt
0.52g

Use good-quality frozen meatballs for these
quick and colorful kebabs.

Meatball Kebabs

12 oz good frozen meatballs, thawed
2 zucchini, cut into chunks
1 red pepper and 1 yellow pepper,
seeded and cut into chunks
6 tbsp honey-mustard dressing
green salad, to serve

Takes 25 minutes • Serves 4

1 Soak eight wooden kebab skewers in water for
15–20 minutes. Put a griddle pan on the stove over
a medium-high heat. While it's heating up, thread
the meatballs onto the skewers with the zucchini
and pepper chunks.
2 Brush them with some of the honey-mustard
dressing. Put the skewers on the hot griddle and
cook for 4–5 minutes on each side (you may need
to do this in batches). Brush them occasionally with
the dressing.
3 Remove the skewers from the pan and serve with
a green salad.

• Per serving: 343 calories, protein 16g, carbohydrate 12g, fat
26g, saturated fat 8g, fiber 4g, added sugar none, salt 1.46g

Red Thai curry paste is a concentrated mixture
of herbs and spices, flavored with dried red chilies.

Thai Red Pork Curry

9oz green beans, trimmed
1 tbsp vegetable oil
4 tsp red Thai curry paste
1 tbsp finely chopped ginger
1lb 2oz boneless pork or beef,
thinly sliced
1 cup vegetable stock
2 tbsp Asian fish sauce
1 tsp light brown sugar
15oz coconut milk
15oz can palm hearts, drained,
rinsed and sliced
grated zest and juice of 1 large lime
handful of fresh basil leaves
handful of fresh cilantro (coriander)
rice noodles, to serve

Takes 35 minutes • Serves 4

1 Cook the green beans in salted boiling water for 5
minutes, then drain and refresh under cold
running water.
2 Heat the oil in a saucepan, add the curry paste
and ginger and saute gently until the oil separates
out. Add the pork and stock, bring to a boil, then
simmer for 5 minutes.
3 Add the fish sauce, sugar, coconut milk, palm
hearts, lime zest and juice and simmer 5 minutes
more, adding the beans halfway through. Throw in
the basil and cilantro and serve with rice noodles.

• Per serving: 396 calories, protein 32g, carbohydrate 10g, fat
26g, saturated fat 16g, fiber 2g, added sugar 1g, salt 2.29g

Use any large smoked sausage, such as German knackwurst or Polish kielbasa. You'll find them with the deli meats.

Smoked Sausage with Leeks

1 tbsp oil
1lb 2oz leeks, trimmed and thickly sliced
1 onion, chopped
salt & pepper to taste
6 tbsp dry white wine
6 tbsp chicken stock
2 large, firm, waxy potatoes, peeled and roughly diced
10oz smoked sausage
3–4 tbsp sour cream
chopped fresh parsley, to garnish

Takes 55 minutes • Serves 2

1 Heat the oil in a large pan, add the leeks and onion and cook for 3–4 minutes, until just softened. Season with salt and pepper, pour in the wine and stock, cover and simmer for 10 minutes.
2 Add the diced potatoes, cover the pan again and simmer for 10 minutes, or until the potatoes are just tender.
3 Prick the sausage with a fork and put it on top of the vegetables. Lower the heat, cover the pan and cook gently for 20 minutes. Lift out the sausage and cut on the diagonal into thick slices. Stir the sour cream into the vegetables and spoon on to plates. Top with the sausage slices and serve garnished with parsley.

• Per serving: 727 calories, protein 29g, carbohydrate 53g, fat 43g, saturated fat 15g, fiber 9g, added sugar none, salt 2.91g

A tasty combination of potatoes, bacon and melted cheese,
much enjoyed by French skiers.

Tartiflette

1lb 10oz potatoes, peeled
1 onion, finely chopped
1oz butter
drizzle of olive oil
6 thick slices bacon
9oz hearty white French cheese
salt & pepper to taste
5oz cream
salad, to serve

Takes 45 minutes • Serves 4

1 Preheat the oven to 425°F. Thickly slice the potatoes, then boil in salted water for 8–10 minutes, until just tender. Drain.

2 Saute the onion in the butter and a drizzle of olive oil for 5 minutes. Snip the bacon into pieces with scissors and add to the pan. Cook for 5 minutes more, until the onion and bacon are lightly browned.

3 Chop the cheese into chunks, rind and all. Layer half the potatoes in a 1-quart buttered ovenproof dish and scatter half the onion, bacon and cheese. Lightly season with salt and pepper. Repeat the layers, pour the cream evenly over the top and bake for 10–12 minutes, until golden. Leave the dish to rest for 5 minutes, and then serve with a salad.

• Per serving: 500 calories, protein 23g, carbohydrate 30g, fat 32g, saturated fat 19g, fiber 2g, added sugar none, salt 2g

There are lots of interesting textures in this tasty
one-pot meal. Serve it with couscous.

Chickpeas with Bacon and Cabbage

1 tbsp oil
1 onion, roughly chopped
4oz slab bacon,
roughly chopped
1 small butternut squash, about
14oz, peeled and cubed
1 cup vegetable or chicken stock
1 tbsp wholegrain mustard
2 × 15oz cans chickpeas, drained
½ green cabbage, shredded
black pepper
couscous, to serve

Takes 50 minutes • Serves 4

1 Heat the oil in a large saucepan. Add the onion
and cook until golden. Add the bacon and cook, stirring, for 5 minutes until beginning to turn crisp.
2 Stir in the squash and stock. Bring to a boil, then
lower the heat and simmer for 15 minutes, stirring
occasionally, until the squash is almost soft.
3 Stir in the mustard, chickpeas and cabbage.
Cover and cook 5 minutes more, until the cabbage
is just cooked. Season with plenty of black pepper
and serve with couscous.

• Per serving: 297 calories, protein 16g, carbohydrate 31g, fat
13g, saturated fat 3g, fiber 9g, added sugar none, salt 1.89g

You can buy ready-made pancakes in most supermarkets, or use leftovers from Sunday breakfast.

Ham and Cheese Pancakes

9oz broccoli, cut into small florets
6 ready-made pancakes
6 smoked ham slices
1 whole 8oz camembert cheese, chilled
salt & pepper to taste
1oz cheddar cheese, grated
4 tomatoes, roughly chopped
salad, to serve

Takes 35 minutes • Serves 4

1 Preheat the oven to 400°F. Cook the broccoli in boiling water for 3 minutes until just tender. Drain and set aside.

2 Put a slice of ham over each pancake. Top with some broccoli. Cut the camembert into thin slices and lay over the broccoli. Season with black pepper. Roll each pancake up like a cigar and place in a single layer in a shallow ovenproof dish.

3 Sprinkle the grated cheddar over the pancakes, then spoon on the chopped tomatoes. Season with salt and pepper and bake for 20 minutes, until the cheese has melted. Serve with a salad.

• Per serving: 379 calories, protein 28g, carbohydrate 11g, fat 25g, saturated fat 14g, fiber 3g, added sugar none, salt 2.3g

You could use the same stuffing for large squash, too.
Cook in the microwave to save time.

Ham-stuffed Eggplant

1 very large or 2 large eggplant,
(about 3lb total)
1oz butter, cut into cubes
salt & pepper to taste
6 tbsp tomato sauce
about 10 slices thinly sliced ham
4 eggs
3oz Double Gloucester or
cheddar cheese, grated

Takes 25 minutes • Serves 4

1 Preheat the oven to 375°F. Peel the eggplant and cut in half lengthwise. Scoop out some of the flesh to make a hollow. Put in a shallow microwave proof dish, dot with butter and season with salt and pepper. Cover with plastic wrap, pierce several times with a fork and cook on High for 7 minutes, until tender.

2 Spoon the tomato sauce into each eggplant half, then arrange the ham on top. Break two eggs into each half and sprinkle with the cheese.

3 Bake for 12–15 minutes, until the eggs are softly set and the cheese has melted and turned golden.

• Per serving: 281 calories, protein 20g, carbohydrate 6g, fat 20g, saturated fat 10g, fiber 1g, added sugar none, salt 2g

For all these flounder recipes, any flatfish will do—
flounder, sole or plaice.

Herb Grilled Flounder

2 tbsp olive oil
1 small shallot, finely chopped
finely grated zest of 1 lemon,
plus 2 tsp lemon juice
2 tsp chopped fresh dill
2 tsp chopped fresh parsley
salt & pepper to taste
2 flounder fillets
steamed new potatoes and peas,
to serve

Takes 25 minutes • Serves 2
(easily doubled)

1 Preheat the broiler. Put the oil and the shallot in a small pan and saute for 2–3 minutes, until the shallot has softened slightly. Stir in the lemon zest and juice and the chopped herbs, and season with salt and pepper.

2 Line the broiler pan with a little oiled foil. Season the fish fillets, then lay them skin-side down on the broiler pan. Spoon the herb oil on top and broil the fish for 5 minutes (there's no need to turn them).

3 Slide the fish on to warm serving plates and pour over the pan juices. Serve with steamed new potatoes and peas.

• Per serving: 230 calories, protein 27g, carbohydrate 1g, fat 13g, saturated fat 2g, fiber trace, added sugar none, salt 0.5g

If you prefer to use cod fillets, add 3–4 minutes to the cooking time, depending on the thickness of the fillets.

Flounder with Bacon Topping

4 thick slices bacon, chopped
olive oil for greasing
4oz fresh white breadcrumbs
grated zest of 1 lemon
2 tbsp chopped fresh parsley
black pepper
4 flounder fillets, about 8oz each
new potatoes and green beans, to serve

Takes 30 minutes • Serves 4

1 Preheat the oven to 450°F. Cook the bacon until crisp. Remove from the heat, pour off most of the bacon fat, and stir in the breadcrumbs, lemon zest and parsley. Season with black pepper.

2 Line a baking sheet with oiled foil and lay the fish fillets on top. Sprinkle the crispy bacon topping over the fish and press down gently.

3 Bake for 7 minutes, or until the fish is cooked and the topping is golden. Serve with new potatoes and green beans.

• Per serving: 305 calories, protein 30g, carbohydrate 19g, fat 13g, saturated fat 3g, fiber 1g, added sugar none, salt 1.55g

Fish will continue to cook once it's out of the oven,
so if you can't serve it immediately, slightly undercook it.

Horseradish-crusted Cod with Lentils

7oz brown lentils
1 small bunch parsley
1 tsp sunflower oil
4 heaped tsp white horseradish
4 × 6oz cod fillets
4 tbsp fresh white breadcrumbs
4 tbsp crème fraîche(or half-and-half
mixed with 1/2 tsp buttermilk)
salt & pepper to taste

Takes 40 minutes • Serves 4

1 Place the lentils in a large saucepan with enough cold water to cover them, plus an extra couple of inches. Add 2 whole sprigs of parsley and bring to a boil. Simmer for 25 minutes or until just tender. Discard the parsley.

2 Meanwhile, preheat the oven to 400°F and grease a non-stick baking tray with the sunflower oil. Lay the bred crumbs on a plate. Spread the horseradish over each fish fillet, then press into the breadcrumbs to coat. Arrange on the baking tray and bake for 15 minutes, until the fish is just cooked through and the breadcrumbs are golden.

3 Meanwhile, roughly chop the remaining parsley. Drain the lentils and toss with the crème fraîche and chopped parsley. Season with salt and pepper and serve with the fish.

• Per serving: 398 calories, protein 47g, carbohydrate 39g, fat 7g, saturated fat 6g, fiber 5g, added sugar 1g, salt 0.86g

Any firm-fleshed fish, such as scrod, haddock, grouper, halibut, snapper or sea bass, can be substituted for cod.

Lemon Cod with Chickpeas

zest and juice of 1 lemon
3 tbsp light olive oil, plus extra
4 × 5oz cod fillets, skinned
salt & pepper to taste
1 onion, sliced into thin wedges
9oz fresh spinach, stems trimmed
½–1 tsp dried chili flakes
16oz can chickpeas, rinsed
and drained

Takes 20 minutes • Serves 4

1 Preheat the broiler. Mix the lemon zest with 1 tablespoon of oil. Line a roasting pan with foil, oil lightly and arrange the fillets on it. Brush with the lemon oil. Season with salt and pepper and broil for 8–10 minutes, until cooked (no need to turn).
2 Meanwhile, heat the rest of the oil and saute the onion until golden. Add the spinach and cook until wilted. Stir in the chili flakes. Add the chickpeas and 1 tablespoon of lemon juice, and heat through. Season with salt and pepper.
3 Spoon the chickpea mixture on to hot plates and place the fish on top. Drizzle with a little extra oil or lemon juice.

• Per serving: 306 calories, protein 32g, carbohydrate 14g, fat 13g, saturated fat 2g, fiber 4g, added sugar none, salt 1.03g

A simple, savory finish for salmon fillets,
cooked in just one pan.

Honey and Soy Salmon

1 tbsp wholegrain mustard
2 tsp honey
1 tbsp soy sauce
1 tsp olive oil
4 skinless salmon fillets,
about 5oz each
3½fl oz vegetable stock
bunch of scallions, cut in half
lengthwise, then cut into strips
rice, to serve

Takes 20 minutes • Serves 4

1 Mix together the mustard, honey and soy sauce in a small bowl. Heat the oil in a frying pan. Add the salmon fillets and cook for 5 minutes, turning halfway through, until almost cooked.

2 Pour the soy mixture over the salmon and bring just to a boil. Add the stock and mix lightly with the pan juices.

3 Sprinkle with the scallion strips and let the liquid bubble for 1–2 minutes, until they are heated through. Serve with boiled rice.

• Per serving: 281 calories, protein 29g, carbohydrate 4g, fat 17g, saturated fat 3g, fiber 1g, added sugar 2g, salt 1.08g

A luxurious dish, deceptively easy
to prepare and perfect for entertaining.

Salmon with Almonds and Cheese

4 × 6oz salmon fillets
salt & pepper to taste
2oz softened butter
4 tbsp slivered or sliced almonds
4 tbsp chopped fresh parsley
2oz gruyère or emmental cheese,
coarsely grated
potatoes and green salad or
broccoli, to serve

Takes 30 minutes • Serves 4

1 Preheat the oven to 375°C. Season the salmon steaks all over with salt and pepper. Liberally butter a shallow ovenproof dish big enough to hold the fish in one layer. Smear the fillets with the remaining butter.
2 Mix together the almonds, parsley and cheese, then press on to the top of the fish.
3 Bake for 15–20 minutes, until the topping is crisp and golden and the salmon is cooked. Serve with potatoes and a green salad or broccoli.

• Per serving: 523 calories, protein 41g, carbohydrate 1g, fat 39g, saturated fat 15g, fiber 1g, added sugar none, salt 0.66g

Whipping cream is rich enough to heat on the stovetop without separating.

Salmon with Tarragon Cream

2 salmon fillets
salt & pepper to taste
1 tbsp vegetable oil
1 finely chopped shallot or
½ small onion
2 tbsp chopped fresh tarragon
6 tbsp whipping cream
2 tbsp chopped fresh parsley
lemon wedges, to garnish
new potatoes and green beans,
to serve

Takes 25 minutes • Serves 2
(easily doubled)

1 Preheat the oven to 350°F. Season the salmon steaks on both sides with salt and pepper. Heat 1 tablespoon of oil in a frying pan (preferably non-stick) until fairly hot. Add the salmon, flesh-side down, and cook quickly for about 3 minutes until lightly browned. Turn over and cook the skin side for 2 minutes.

2 Transfer to a shallow ovenproof dish and sprinkle with the shallot and the tarragon. Spoon on the cream and season with salt and pepper.

3 Cook in the oven for 12–15 minutes, until the salmon is cooked. Sprinkle with chopped parsley, transfer to warm plates and garnish with lemon wedges. Serve with new potatoes and green beans.

• Per serving: 448 calories, protein 32g, carbohydrate 3g, fat 34g, saturated fat 14g, fiber 1g, added sugar none, salt 0.23g

As a variation, instead of the garlic and herb soft cheese, try using the black pepper variety.

Salmon Watercress Puffs

2–3oz watercress
13oz frozen puff pastry, thawed
4 skinless salmon fillets, 5oz each
grated zest of 1 lemon
salt & pepper to taste
5oz soft cheese with garlic
and herbs
milk or beaten egg, for brushing
new potatoes, to serve

Takes 30 minutes • Serves 4

1 Preheat the oven to 400°F. Put half the watercress in a pan with 1 tablespoon of water and cook for a few minutes until wilted. Drain and chop.
2 Roll out the pastry to a 15 × 12-inch rectangle. Cut in quarters to make four smaller rectangles. Put a salmon fillet on one half of each rectangle. Scatter over a little lemon zest and season with salt and pepper. Divide the cheese and cooked watercress between the fillets. Dampen the pastry edges with a little milk or egg, fold over the pastry and seal to enclose the filling.
3 Put the pastry parcels on a baking sheet and brush with milk or egg. Bake for 20 minutes, until the pastry is puffed and golden. Serve with the remaining watercress and new potatoes.

• Per serving: 675 calories, protein 38g, carbohydrate 36g, fat 43g, saturated fat 3g, fiber trace, added sugar none, salt 1.21g

Choose a salad that contains radicchio and a mixture
of white and red cabbage to give this dish a lovely crunch.

Salmon and Salad Stir Fry

1 tbsp oil
2in piece fresh ginger, grated
salt & pepper to taste
1lb salmon fillet, skinned and
cut into 1in cubes
bunch of scallions, cut into
1½in lengths
½ cup vegetable stock
6oz mesclun or mixed leafy
vegetables
2 tbsp light soy sauce
rice, to serve

Takes 25 minutes • Serves 4

1 Heat the oil in a frying pan, add the ginger and
cook for 30 seconds, stirring. Season the salmon
with salt and pepper, add to the pan and cook for
5 minutes, turning once until just cooked through
and beginning to brown.

2 Remove the salmon from the pan and keep warm.
Add the scallions and stir fry for 3–4 minutes, until
just soft.

3 Pour in the stock and bring to a boil. Add the vegetables and cook for 1 minute to wilt. Return the
salmon to the pan, add the soy sauce and serve hot
from the pan with rice.

• Per serving: 248 calories, protein 24g, carbohydrate 3g, fat
16g, saturated fat 3g, fiber 1g, added sugar none, salt 0.26g

Don't miss out on trout because you don't like bones.
Fillets are easy to eat with salad.

Trout with Warm Potato Salad

1lb 5oz new potatoes
8oz broccoli, cut into small florets
4 trout fillets, about 4oz each
3 tbsp olive oil, plus extra
for brushing
salt & pepper to taste
1 tbsp white wine vinegar
12 cherry tomatoes, halved
2 tbsp toasted sliced almonds

Takes 20 minutes • Serves 4

1 Wash the potatoes and cut each in half, or quarters if large. Cook in salted boiling water for 12 minutes, adding the broccoli for the last 3 minutes of cooking time.
2 Preheat the broiler. Put the trout fillets in a broiler pan. Brush each with a little oil and season with salt and pepper. Broil for 3–4 minutes.
3 Drain the potatoes and broccoli well. Put in a bowl. Whisk together the 3 tablespoons of oil and the vinegar. Add to the hot vegetables, along with the tomatoes, almonds and a little salt and pepper. Toss well and serve with the broiled trout.

• Per serving: 378 calories, protein 26g, carbohydrate 26g, fat 19g, saturated fat 2g, fiber 4g, added sugar none, salt 0.43g

The perfect late-night snack for one.
Or multiply the recipe for a weekend family brunch.

Smoked Salmon Muffins

1 English muffin
knob of unsalted butter, plus
extra for buttering
2 eggs
1 tbsp milk
black pepper
1oz smoked salmon pieces
1 tsp freshly chopped chives

Takes 10 minutes • Serves 1

1 Preheat the broiler. Split and toast the muffin until golden. Spread with butter and keep warm. Meanwhile, lightly beat the eggs and milk together in a bowl and season with freshly ground black pepper.
2 Melt the butter in a pan and, when foaming, pour in the eggs. Cook over a low heat, pulling the cooked egg from the edges of the pan into the center until the egg begins to set.
3 Stir in the smoked salmon and chives and cook 1–2 minutes more. Pile on top of the toasted muffin halves and serve.

• Per serving: 502 calories, protein 26g, carbohydrate 34g, fat 30g, saturated fat 13g, fiber 1g, added sugar none, salt 2.39g

This easy family meal cooks wonderfully—
and quickly—in the microwave.

Smoked Haddock with Chive Potatoes

2lb 2oz potatoes
1 small onion, thinly sliced
salt & pepper to taste
1oz butter
1 cup vegetable stock
5oz frozen peas
5oz cream
4 boneless, skinless smoked
haddock fillets, about 5oz each
2 tbsp freshly chopped chives

Takes 30 minutes • Serves 4

1 Peel and thickly slice the potatoes. Put into a large microwave proof shallow dish, about 2-quart capacity, with the onion, and season with salt and pepper. Dot with half the butter and pour on the stock.

2 Cover loosely with plastic wrap and microwave on High for 15 minutes, stirring halfway through, until the potatoes are just tender. Gently stir in the peas and pour over the cream.

3 Put the smoked haddock on top of the potatoes and dot each piece with the remaining butter. Sprinkle with the chives. Cover with plastic wrap and cook for 5 minutes on High, until the fish is just cooked through. Serve immediately.

• Per serving: 413 calories, protein 34g, carbohydrate 41g, fat 14g, saturated fat 8g, fiber 5g, added sugar none, salt 3.15g

Use raw king prawns to make this simple
but extra-special supper.

Gently Spiced Shrimp Curry

10 raw jumbo shrimp, in their shells
4 tsp vegetable oil
1 tsp mustard seeds
1 small onion, finely chopped
1 tbsp finely chopped fresh ginger
1 plump garlic clove, finely chopped
¼ tsp ground turmeric
¼ tsp hot chili powder
½ tsp ground coriander
2 fresh bay leaves
1 small green chili, seeded and
thinly sliced
7oz sweetened condensed
coconut milk
1 lime, halved
salt to taste
basmati rice and lime wedges,
to serve

Takes 30 minutes • Serves 2

1 Peel the shrimp and set aside. Heat the oil in a medium frying pan. Cook the mustard seeds until they crackle and pop. Add the onion. Stir fry, stirring, until golden. Add the ginger and garlic. Stir fry for 1 minute.

2 Add the turmeric, chili powder and coriander and stir fry for 30 seconds. Add the bay leaves and chili. Stir over medium heat for 1 minute. Pour in ½ cup water and let bubble for a minute.

3 Add the shrimp and spoon on the sauce. Lower the heat and simmer for 3–4 minutes, until the shrimp is cooked. Pour in the coconut milk, warm through and squeeze in the juice of half a lime. Season with salt. Serve with basmati rice and lime wedges.

• Per serving: 519 calories, protein 23g, carbohydrate 12g, fat 42g, saturated fat 31g, fiber 1g, added sugar none, salt 3.08g

Shrimp and eggs are a surprisingly successful combination.
Try this for a late supper for two.

Shrimp and Scallion Omelette

1 tbsp olive oil
4 eggs
salt & pepper to taste
4oz peeled, cooked shrimp
4 scallions, trimmed and
thinly sliced
tomato salad and crusty bread,
to serve

Takes 10 minutes • Serves 2
(easily doubled)

1 Preheat the broiler. Heat the oil in a frying pan. Lightly beat the eggs and season with salt and pepper. Pour into the frying pan and cook over medium heat for 30 seconds until the egg mixture starts to set.
2 Using a fork, gently draw some of the egg mixture from the edge of the pan into the middle. Scatter the shrimp and scallions in the pan and cook for 2 minutes.
3 Transfer the pan to the broiler and cook 1–2 minutes more, until golden brown. Fold the omelette over. Cut in half and serve with a tomato salad and crusty bread.

• Per serving: 250 calories, protein 24g, carbohydrate none, fat 17g, saturated fat 4g, fiber none, added sugar none, salt 1.36g

This is a snap to make—ready-made pancakes and a
sauce made from a can of soup make it simplicity itself.

Seafood Pancakes

1oz butter
1 onion, chopped
2 celery stalks, chopped
1 tbsp all-purpose flour
15oz can cream of spinach soup,
mixed with ½ can of milk
5oz heavy cream
1lb 9oz mixture of fresh fish,
such as cod and salmon,
cut into chunks, and seafood
such as shrimp and mussels
black pepper
12 ready-made pancakes
2oz sharp cheddar cheese, grated

Takes 40 minutes • Serves 6

1 Preheat the oven to 400°F. Heat the butter in a pan and saute the onion and celery for 5 minutes until softened. Stir in the flour and cook for 1 minute more. Add half the soup mixture and half the cream. Bring to a boil.

2 Add the fish and simmer for 5 minutes, stirring gently, until the fish is just cooked. Season with black pepper. Spoon the mixture into the center of the pancakes and fold into square parcels. Arrange in a shallow ovenproof dish.

3 Heat the remaining soup and cream, spoon over the pancakes, and sprinkle with the cheese. Bake for 20–25 minutes until the cheese is golden.

• Per serving: 571 calories, protein 28g, carbohydrate 28g, fat 39g, saturated fat 20g, fiber 2g, added sugar none, salt 1.99g

Syllabub is a milk punch. Don't over-whip the cream or it will be too stiff to mix easily with the meringue and fruit.

Raspberry Syllabub Mess

3 ready-made meringues
12oz fresh raspberries
4 tbsp dry white wine
3oz fine sugar
finely grated zest and juice
of 1 lemon
10oz heavy cream
confectioner's sugar, for dusting

Takes 10 minutes • Serves 4

1 Break the meringues into pieces in a bowl. Add 9oz raspberries.

2 In a large bowl, stir together the wine, sugar, lemon zest and juice, until the sugar has dissolved. Using a wire whisk, gradually whisk in the cream, until it just holds its shape.

3 Spoon the syllabub over the meringue and raspberries and gently mix. Do not overmix or the cream will turn pink. Spoon into a serving bowl, scatter with the remaining raspberries and chill. Dust with confectioner's sugar just before serving.

• Per serving: 502 calories, protein 3g, carbohydrate 46g, fat 34g, saturated fat 21g, fiber 2g, added sugar 39g, salt 0.12g

Use a potato peeler to make shavings from a
thick chocolate bar.

Chocolate Cream Pots

5oz dark chocolate
5oz whipping cream
5 tbsp Irish cream liqueur
8oz mascarpone cheese
chocolate shavings,
to decorate (optional)

Takes 20 minutes • Serves 4

1 Break the chocolate into a bowl and microwave
on High for about 2 minutes, or until melted.
Alternatively, melt in a bowl set over simmering
water, making sure the bottom of the bowl doesn't
touch the water. Stir and set aside to cool.
2 Whisk the cream to soft peaks and whisk in the
Irish cream liqueur. Beat the mascarpone until
smooth, then beat into the Irish cream liqueur mixture. Pour in the cooled chocolate and stir lightly to
make a swirly pattern.
3 Spoon the mixture into small bowls or teacups.
Cover generously with chocolate shavings, and
serve.

• Per serving: 703 calories, protein 5g, carbohydrate 37g, fat
59g, saturated fat 34g, fiber 1g, added sugar 32g, salt 0.24g

A really quick dessert combining no-cook ingredients.
Try it with other fruits too.

Apricot Cookies 'n' Cream

15oz can apricots in natural juice
9oz heavy cream
6 oz plain, mild yogurt
10 chocolate cookies or plain
cookies coated with chocolates
1 tsp ground cinnamon
2 tbsp raw sugar

Takes 10 minutes • Serves 4

1 Drain the apricots, reserving half of the juice. Roughly chop the apricots and divide among four glasses. Spoon on the reserved juice.

2 In a bowl, mix together the cream and yogurt. Roughly chop the cookies and stir into the cream mixture, then spoon over the apricots.

3 Mix together the cinnamon and sugar. Sprinkle over the cream mixture and serve immediately.

• Per serving: 649 calories, protein 8g, carbohydrate 47g, fat 49g, saturated fat 29g, fiber 2g, added sugar 19g, salt 0.66g

An easily assembled dessert. Make it more grown up by adding a little kirsch or brandy to the cherry syrup.

Black Forest Trifle

6oz fruitcake cake
16oz can pitted black cherries in syrup
3oz chocolate shavings
3oz semisweet chocolate chips
16oz can or carton fresh custard
6oz crème fraîche (or heavy cream with 1/2 tsp buttermilk)

Takes 20 minutes, plus chilling • Serves 4 generously

1 Cut the cake into thick slices and use to line the base of a 2-quart serving bowl. Cut three cherries in half and reserve, and spoon the rest over the cake along with the syrup. Crumble half the shaved chocolate over the cherries and scatter half the chocolate chips.

2 Heat the remaining chocolate chips in a microwave proof bowl on Medium for 2 minutes, stirring halfway through, until melted. Cool for 5 minutes, then gradually whisk into the custard, until you have a smooth chocolate custard. Pour over the cherries.

3 Spoon the crème fraîche over the custard. Sprinkle with the reserved cherries and crumble on the remaining flake. Chill until ready to serve.

• Per serving: 478 calories, protein 7g, carbohydrate 59g, fat 25g, saturated fat 14g, fiber 1g, added sugar 16g, salt 0.57g

An instant iced dessert, guaranteed to
make a refreshing finale to a meal.

Summer Fruits Ice Yogurt

16oz frozen mixed summer fruits
12oz carton plain, mild yogurt
3½fl oz (about 7 tbsp) fresh
orange juice
1 tbsp confectioner's sugar
cookies, shortbread or vanilla
wafers, to serve (optional)

Takes 10 minutes • Serves 4

1 Put the frozen fruits, yogurt, orange juice and
confectioner's sugar in a food processor. Process
until blended, but make sure the fruit still has some
texture.
2 Scrape the mixture from the sides of the
workbowl and process again. Repeat until the
mixture looks like frozen yogurt.
3 Spoon into wide glasses and serve immediately,
with cookies, if you like.

• Per serving: 184 calories, protein 8g, carbohydrate 18g, fat
9g, saturated fat 6g, fiber 3g, added sugar 7g, salt 0.2g

Keep the heat quite high during the cooking so
the sugar melts to produce a sticky sauce.

Fried Rum Bananas

knob of butter
4 bananas, sliced on the diagonal
into four pieces
4 tbsp rum or brandy
4 tbsp heavy cream
2 tbsp light brown sugar

Takes 10 minutes • Serves 4

1 Melt the butter in a large frying pan. When the butter is foaming, fry the bananas for 2 minutes, then turn them and pour in the rum or brandy. Fry for 1–2 minutes, more until browned.
2 Stir the cream and sugar into the pan and warm through for 1 minute.
3 Divide the bananas among four plates and spoon over the sauce. Serve immediately.

• Per serving: 237 calories, protein 2g, carbohydrate 32g, fat 9g, saturated fat 5g, fiber 1g, added sugar 8g, salt 0.11g

A sweet and gooey open sandwich made in 10 minutes
from ingredients you probably have in the pantry.

Choc-o-nut Pear Toasts

1oz butter
2 pears, peeled, cored and sliced
1oz light brown sugar
juice of 1 orange
4 thick slices white bread
4 tbsp chocolate nut spread
(such as Nutella)

Takes 10 minutes • Serves 4

1 Preheat the broiler. Melt the butter in a frying pan, then add the pear slices and fry quickly for about 5 minutes, until lightly browned and softened.
2 Stir in the sugar, then add the orange juice and let it bubble until it forms a syrupy sauce.
3 Toast the bread on both sides. Spoon the chocolate nut spread over one side of each slice of bread. Put on serving plates and spoon onto the hot pears. Serve immediately.

• Per serving: 262 calories, protein 4g, carbohydrate 36g, fat 12g, saturated fat 4g, fiber 2g, added sugar 7g, salt 0.52g

Try nectarines or peaches served warm for a change.
You'll love this combination of fruit and cream cheese.

Roasted Stuffed Nectarines

4 nectarines
8 gingersnaps
1oz butter
2 tsp honey
finely grated zest and juice
of 1 orange
8oz softened cream cheese cheese
2 tbsp fine sugar

Takes 25 minutes • Serves 4

1 Preheat the oven to 350°F. Halve the nectarines and remove and discard the pits. Put the nectarines flesh-side up in a shallow, ovenproof dish.
2 Put the cookies in a plastic bag and roughly crush with a rolling pin. Melt the butter in a small pan over low heat. Stir the crushed cookies into the melted butter, along with the honey. Spoon a little of the mixture on top of each nectarine.
3 Pour the orange juice over the nectarines and bake for 20 minutes. Meanwhile, put the cream cheese in a bowl and beat in the sugar and orange zest. Serve with the warm nectarines and pan juices.

• Per serving: 416 calories, protein 8g, carbohydrate 43g, fat 25g, saturated fat 4g, fiber 3g, added sugar 14g, salt 1g

Based on the baked Alaska idea—baked ice cream
and meringue—but using a moist ginger cake.

Baked Jamaica

8oz can pineapple chunks in
natural juice
1 store-bought ginger cake (or
sponge cake), sliced horizontally
3 egg whites
6oz light brown sugar
16oz vanilla ice cream, removed
from the carton in a block

Takes 20 minutes • Serves 4

1 Preheat the oven to 425°F. Drain the pineapple,
reserving 3 tablespoons of juice. Put the ginger cake
slices side by side in a rectangular shallow
ovenproof dish. Drizzle over the pineapple juice and
pineapple chunks.
2 Whisk the egg whites until stiff. Whisk in the
sugar, a tablespoon at a time, whisking well between
each addition until the meringue is thick and glossy.
3 Slice the ice cream and cover the fruit and cake
with it, pressing down to make it level. Completely
cover with the meringue, swirling the top with a fork.
Bake for 5 minutes until golden. Serve at once.

• Per serving: 484 calories, protein 9g, carbohydrate 85g, fat
14g, saturated fat 7g, fiber 1g, added sugar 59g, salt 0.53g

Try this easy-mix crumble topping with other fruits, too.
A microwave speeds cooking but is not essential.

Red Fruit Oat Crumble

4 apples, such as macintosh,
peeled, cored and chopped
10oz can summer fruits in syrup
4oz butter
2oz light brown sugar
5oz whole oats
ready-made custard, ice cream or
whipping cream, to serve

Takes 40 minutes • Serves 4

1 Preheat the oven to 375°F. Mix together the apples, summer fruits and their syrup in a 1-quart microwave proof pie pan. Microwave on High for 5–8 minutes, stirring halfway through, until the apples are cooked. Alternatively, cook in a pan on the stove, stirring, for 12–15 minutes.
2 Melt the butter in a bowl on Medium in the microwave for 1–2 minutes (or in a small pan), until just melted. Stir in the sugar and oats. Spoon over the fruit.
3 Bake for 20 minutes, until the topping is golden and the filling is just bubbling. Serve with custard, ice cream or cream.

• Per serving: 478 calories, protein 5g, carbohydrate 65g, fat 24g, saturated fat 14g, fiber 5g, added sugar 19g, salt 0.56g

Index

Picture credits and recipe credits

BBC Worldwide would like to thank the following for providing photographs. While every effort has been made to trace and acknowledge all photographers, we would like to apologise should there be any errors or omissions.

Marie-Louise Avery p69, p113, p191; Iain Bagwell p31, p143; Jean Cazals p17, p55, p79; Ken Field p19, p37, p41, p97, p111, p149; David Jordan p27; David Munns p33, p39, p99, p165; William Reavell p23; Craig Robertson p45, p103, p193; Simon Smith p35, p43, p91, p179; Roger Stowell p13, p15, p25, p29, p47, p49, p51, p53, p57, p61, p67, p73, p75, p83, p85, p95, p101, p105, p107, p109, p115, p117, p119, p121, p123, p129, p131, p135, p139, p141, p145, p151, p153, p159, p161, p163, p167, p169, p175, p177, p181, p185, p189, p197, p199, p201, p203, p205, p207, p209, p211; Sam Stowell p93, p171; Martin Thompson p125, p157; Martin Thompson and Philip Webb p127; Ian Wallace p195; Philip Webb p21, p63, p187; Simon Wheeler p65, p71, p77, p81, p87, p133, p137, p147, p155, p173; Jonathan Whittaker p11, p59, p89; Geoff Wilkinson p183

All the recipes in this book have been created by the editorial teams on *BBC Good Food Magazine* and *BBC Vegetarian Good Food Magazine*.

Angela Boggiano, Lorna Brash, Sara Buenfeld, Mary Cadogan, Gilly Cubitt, Barney Desmazery, Joanna Farrow, Rebecca Ford, Silvana Franco, Catherine Hill, Jane Lawrie, Clare Lewis, Sara Lewis, Liz Martin, Kate Moseley, Orlando Murrin, Vicky Musselman, Angela Nilsen, Justine Pattison, Jenny White and Jeni Wright.